First World War
and Army of Occupation
War Diary
France, Belgium and Germany

21 DIVISION
62 Infantry Brigade
Lincolnshire Regiment
2nd Battalion
1 February 1918 - 31 March 1919

WO95/2154/2

The Naval & Military Press Ltd
www.nmarchive.com
Published in association with The National Archives

Published by

The Naval & Military Press Ltd

Unit 10 Ridgewood Industrial Park,
Uckfield, East Sussex,
TN22 5QE England
Tel: +44 (0) 1825 749494

www.naval-military-press.com

www.nmarchive.com

This diary has been reprinted in facsimile from the original. Any imperfections are inevitably reproduced and the quality may fall short of modern type and cartographic standards.

© **Crown Copyright**
Images reproduced by permission of The National Archives, London, England, 2015.

Contents

Document type	Place/Title	Date From	Date To
Heading	WO95/2154/2		
Heading	21st Division 62nd Infy Bde 2nd Bn Lincolnshire Regt Feb 1918-Mar 1919 WO95/2154 From 8 Div 25 Bde		
War Diary	Watou	01/02/1918	04/02/1918
War Diary	Haut-Allaines	05/02/1918	07/02/1918
War Diary	Gurlu Wood	08/02/1918	18/02/1918
War Diary	Moislains	19/02/1918	28/02/1918
Heading	62nd Inf Bde. 21st Div. War Diary 2nd Battn. The Lincolnshire Regiment. March 1918		
Miscellaneous	D.A.G. Base.	20/04/1918	20/04/1918
War Diary	Heudicourt	19/03/1918	22/03/1918
War Diary	Gurlu Wood	23/03/1918	23/03/1918
War Diary	Heudicourt	01/03/1918	06/03/1918
War Diary	Bn. Head Qrs Dug-Out At W18.c.9.5	07/03/1918	18/03/1918
War Diary	Gurlu Wood	23/03/1918	23/03/1918
War Diary	Near Clery	24/03/1918	24/03/1918
War Diary	Suzanne	25/03/1918	25/03/1918
War Diary	Chipilly	26/03/1918	26/03/1918
War Diary	Bresle	27/03/1918	27/03/1918
War Diary	Beaucourt	28/03/1918	29/03/1918
War Diary	Bonnay	30/03/1918	30/03/1918
War Diary	Poulainville	31/03/1918	31/03/1918
Miscellaneous	Appendices.		
Operation(al) Order(s)	62nd Infantry Brigade Order No. 74	17/03/1918	17/03/1918
Miscellaneous	B.M. 68/77	18/03/1918	18/03/1918
Miscellaneous	Report On Raid Carried Out By C. Company 2nd Bn Lincolnshire Regt On Night 13/19th March 1918	13/03/1918	13/03/1918
Miscellaneous	2nd Bn Lincolnshire Regiment. List of Casualties From 21.3.18 To 2.4.18	21/03/1918	21/03/1918
Heading	62nd Brigade. 21st Division. 2nd Battalion Lincolnshire Regiment April 1918		
War Diary	Hangest	01/04/1918	01/04/1918
War Diary	Peselhoek	02/04/1918	02/04/1918
War Diary	Kemmel	03/04/1918	04/04/1918
War Diary	Wytschaete	06/04/1918	07/04/1918
War Diary	Kemmel Shelters.	08/04/1918	10/04/1918
War Diary	Wytschaete	11/04/1918	17/04/1918
War Diary	Siege Farm	18/04/1918	20/04/1918
War Diary	Scottish Camp	20/04/1918	25/04/1918
War Diary	Near Dickebusch	26/04/1918	30/04/1918
Miscellaneous	2nd Bn Lincolnshire Regiment. List of Casualties		
Miscellaneous	2nd Lincolnshire Regiment. Account of Operations from 10th April to 19th April 1918	10/04/1918	10/04/1918
Heading	2nd Battalion Lincolnshire Regiment. War Diary. Period. 1st May 1918. To 31st May 1918		
War Diary	Camp Nr Busse Boom	01/05/1918	01/05/1918
War Diary	Beauvoorde	02/05/1918	02/05/1918
War Diary	Lederzeele	03/05/1918	05/05/1918
War Diary	In Train	06/05/1918	07/05/1918
War Diary	Lhery	08/05/1918	12/05/1918

War Diary	Nr Bouvancourt	13/05/1918	13/05/1918
War Diary	Camp "A"	14/05/1918	14/05/1918
War Diary	Chalons Le Verguer	14/05/1918	20/05/1918
War Diary	Chalons-Le-Verguer	21/05/1918	21/05/1918
War Diary	Front Line Trenches	22/05/1918	27/05/1918
War Diary	Pevy	28/05/1918	28/05/1918
War Diary	Nr Prouilly	28/05/1918	28/05/1918
War Diary	Near Muizon	29/05/1918	29/05/1918
War Diary	Mery-Premecy	30/05/1918	30/05/1918
War Diary	Vauciennes	31/05/1918	31/05/1918
Miscellaneous	2nd Battalion Lincolnshire Regiment. List of Casualties.	05/06/1918	05/06/1918
Heading	2nd Battalion Lincolnshire Regiment. War Diary. Period. 1st June 1918 To 30th June 1918. Vol 44		
War Diary	Soulieres	01/06/1918	03/06/1918
War Diary	Villevenard	04/06/1918	09/06/1918
War Diary	Beauvais	10/06/1918	14/06/1918
War Diary	En Route	15/06/1918	15/06/1918
War Diary	Hallencourt	16/06/1918	17/06/1918
War Diary	Aumatre	18/06/1918	21/06/1918
War Diary	Bazinval	22/06/1918	22/06/1918
War Diary	Melleville	23/06/1918	30/06/1918
Map			
Heading	2nd Battalion Lincolnshire Regt War Diary For Period 1st To 31st July 1918 Vol 45		
War Diary	Melleville	01/07/1918	01/07/1918
War Diary	Beauquesne	02/07/1918	14/07/1918
War Diary	Toutencourt	15/07/1918	18/07/1918
War Diary	Raincheval	19/07/1918	24/07/1918
War Diary	Near Mailly-Maillet	28/07/1918	31/07/1918
Operation(al) Order(s)	2nd Battn Lincolnshire Regiment. Operation Order No. 42. Appendix No 1	14/07/1918	14/07/1918
Operation(al) Order(s)	2nd Battn Lincolnshire Regt Battn Operation Order No 43. Appendix No II	17/07/1918	17/07/1918
Operation(al) Order(s)	2nd Battn Lincolnshire Regt Battn Operation Order No 44. Appendix No III	24/07/1918	24/07/1918
Operation(al) Order(s)	2nd Battn Lincolnshire Regt Battn Operation Order No 45. Appendix No IV	28/07/1918	28/07/1918
Miscellaneous	Distribution		
Map	German Trenches In Blue Trenches Revised From Information Received To 28-7-18		
Heading	War Diary Of The 2nd Bn Lincolnshire Regiment From-1st August 1918 To-31st August 1918		
War Diary	Mailly-Maillet.	01/08/1918	08/08/1918
War Diary	Beaussart	09/08/1918	09/08/1918
War Diary	Mailly-Maillet.	10/08/1918	16/08/1918
War Diary	Y Ravine Q.10.d.6.7	17/08/1918	20/08/1918
War Diary	Nr Auchonvillers	20/08/1918	21/08/1918
War Diary	Luminous Avenue.	21/08/1918	21/08/1918
War Diary	Ravine, R.I.d.6.8	22/08/1918	24/08/1918
War Diary	Boom Valley, R. 11.c.1.4	24/08/1918	25/08/1918
War Diary	1000 Yards Le Sars.	25/08/1918	25/08/1918
War Diary	East Of Le Sars.	25/08/1918	25/08/1918
War Diary	N. Of Le Sars.	26/08/1918	26/08/1918
War Diary	Butte De Warlencourt	27/08/1918	27/08/1918
War Diary	Warlencourt	28/08/1918	31/08/1918
Miscellaneous	Total Casualties During The Month Of August, 1918		

Type	Description	Date From	Date To
Heading	Cover for Documents. Nature of Enclosures. War Diary of 2nd Bn Lincolnshire Regiment for Period 1st September 1918 to 30th September 1918. Vol 43		
War Diary	Warlencourt	01/09/1918	01/09/1918
War Diary	N.E. Of Le Sars	02/09/1918	02/09/1918
War Diary	S.E. of Guedecourt.	03/09/1918	04/09/1918
War Diary	N.W. Of Rocquigny	05/09/1918	05/09/1918
War Diary	S.E. Of Manancourt.	06/09/1918	06/09/1918
War Diary	N.W. of Elsom Copse	06/09/1918	06/09/1918
War Diary	V.23.a.0.8	07/09/1918	07/09/1918
War Diary	S. Of Heudecourt	07/09/1918	09/09/1918
War Diary	Manancourt	10/09/1918	16/09/1918
War Diary	S. Of Heudecourt	16/09/1918	18/09/1918
War Diary	W.22.b.5.O	18/09/1918	19/09/1918
War Diary	W.24.c.3.O.	19/09/1918	19/09/1918
War Diary	N Of Nurlu.	20/09/1918	20/09/1918
War Diary	W. Of Le Mesnil	21/09/1918	25/09/1918
War Diary	W. Of Gouzeaucourt	26/09/1918	29/09/1918
War Diary	Railway East Of Gonnelieu.	30/09/1918	30/09/1918
Miscellaneous	Since August 21st, 1918, The Following Awards For Gallantry In Action Have Been Made To Officers, N.C.O.'s And Men Of The Battalion.		
Operation(al) Order(s)	62nd Infantry Brigade Order No. 18	16/09/1918	16/09/1918
Operation(al) Order(s)	Appendix "B" To 62nd Inf Bde. Order No. 18		
Operation(al) Order(s)	Appendix "C" To 62nd Inf Bde. Order No. 18		
Operation(al) Order(s)	Appendix "F" To 62nd Inf Bde. Order No. 18		
Operation(al) Order(s)	Appendix "G" To 62nd Inf Bde. Order No. 18		
Operation(al) Order(s)	Appendix "D" To 62nd Inf Bde. Order No. 18		
Operation(al) Order(s)	Appendix "E" To 62nd Inf Bde. Order No. 18		
Miscellaneous	Summary Of Prisoners Etc.		
Operation(al) Order(s)	Appendix "A" To 62nd Infantry Brigade Order No. 18		
Map	Barrage Map Issued With 21 D.A. O.O No. 5		
Map	2nd Lincolnshire Regiment Attack On Sept. 18th 1918		
Miscellaneous	Message Form.		
Map	Enemy Organisation 21-8-18		
Miscellaneous	Appendix C		
Map			
Heading	WO95/2155 Appendix D (b)		
Map			
Heading	WO95/2154 Appendix D (a)		
Map	German Trenches In Blue. Trenches Revised From Information Received To 20-8-18		
Miscellaneous	57 Co RE		
Map	Corps Topo Outline Reference.		
Miscellaneous	Message Form.		
Heading	War Diary Of 2nd Battalion The Lincolnshire Regiment From-1st October 1918. To 31st October 1918. Vol 48		
War Diary	E of Gonnelieu	01/10/1918	03/10/1918
War Diary	Q 34a4.5	04/10/1918	05/10/1918
War Diary	R 33c8.6	06/10/1918	07/10/1918
War Diary	S5.b.9.5	08/10/1918	08/10/1918
War Diary	N 33a.9.6	09/10/1918	09/10/1918
War Diary	N30a15.50	10/10/1918	10/10/1918
War Diary	Walincourt	11/10/1918	22/10/1918
War Diary	Inchy	22/10/1918	31/10/1918
Map	Appendix V		

Miscellaneous			
Heading	62nd Bde 21 Div War Diary 1st Bn. Lincolnshire Regt November 1918		
Heading	War Diary Volume II Of The 2nd Bn Lincolnshire Regiment For Period 1st November 1918 To 30th November 1918. Vol 49		
War Diary	Poix du Nord	01/11/1918	02/11/1918
War Diary	Vendegies Au Bois (F.7.8. & 13.)	02/11/1918	04/11/1918
War Diary	Les Tuileries Futoy	04/11/1918	04/11/1918
War Diary	Forest De Mormal	04/11/1918	05/11/1918
War Diary	1 a Tete Noire Berlaimont	05/11/1918	05/11/1918
War Diary	Berlaimont	05/11/1918	07/11/1918
War Diary	Aymeries	07/11/1918	11/11/1918
War Diary	Bachant	12/11/1918	23/11/1918
War Diary	Bachant	22/11/1918	29/11/1918
Operation(al) Order(s)	1st Battn The Lincolnshire Regiment Operation Order No 158 By Lt. Col. N.M.S. Irwin D.S.O. M.C. Commdg. Appendix I	03/11/1918	03/11/1918
Operation(al) Order(s)	1st Battn The Lincolnshire Regiment Operation Order No 157 By Lt. Col. N. M. S. Irwin D.S.O. M.C. Commdg.	03/11/1918	03/11/1918
Map	Appendix 2		
Map	Legende		
Miscellaneous			
Heading	War Diary (Volume 12) Of 2nd Bn Lincolnshire Regiment For Period 1st December 1918 To 31st December 1918 Vol 50		
War Diary	Bachant	01/12/1918	17/12/1918
War Diary	Engle-Fontaine.	18/12/1918	18/12/1918
War Diary	Inchy	18/12/1918	19/12/1918
War Diary	Saisseval	19/12/1918	31/12/1918
Heading	War Diary Of The 2nd Battn Lincolnshire Regt For Period 1st January 1919 To 31st January 1919		
War Diary	Saisseval	01/01/1919	31/01/1919
Heading	War Diary Of The 2nd Bn Lincolnshire Rgt For Period 1st February 1919 To 28th February 1919 (Volume 2) Lieut Colonel Commdg 2nd Bn Lincolnshire Rgt.		
War Diary	Saisseval	01/02/1919	28/02/1919
Heading	War Diary Of The 2nd. Bn. Lincolnshire Regt. For Period 1st. March 1919 To 31st March 1919. Volume 3		
War Diary	Saisseval.	01/03/1919	06/03/1919
War Diary	Cavillon.	07/03/1919	31/03/1919
Heading	1 Lincoln Regt Vol XVII		
Heading	1 Lincoln Regt Vol 19		
Heading	1 Lincoln Regt Vol XIX		
Miscellaneous			

W0052154/2

21ST DIVISION
62ND INFY BDE

2ND BN LINCOLNSHIRE REGT
FEB 1918 — MAR 1919

WO95/2154

From 8 DIV 25 BDE

WAR DIARY or **INTELLIGENCE SUMMARY**

Army Form C. 2118.

2nd R. Inniskilling Regt.

Place	Date	Hour	Summary of Events and Information	Remarks and references to Appendices.
MATOU	1-2-18		Batt. in Divisional Rest Area. Musketry, Training &c.	
"	2--			
"	3--		Batt. moves to join the 21st Division. Route N°16 at 6.18 to GODEWAERSVELDE by march route, from GODEWAERSVELDE to PERONNE by train. The Batt. entrained at 10.30 pm 3/2 and detrained at 4 am 4-2-18. From PERONNE the Batt. marched to billets at HAUT-ALLAINES to form part of 62nd Infy Brigade to which the 1st Bn of the Regt already belonged.	
"	4--			
HAUT-ALLAINES	5--		Re-organisation and Training. The Bn was addressed by the Divisional General at 12.15 pm on the 6-2-18	
"	6--			
"	7--	8 am	Bn marched from HAUT-ALLAINES to GURLU WOOD Sh 62c D.3.2. for work on GREEN LINE. Army Defense Zone, relieving the 9th Bn K.O.Y.L.I.	
GURLU WOOD	8--		Work on GREEN LINE. Digging Mining &c, and training of specialists	
"	9--		Enemy aircraft bombed the vicinity of the camp on the night 11-12-18 killing one man.	
GREEN WOOD	13--		Bn moves to MOISLAINS and takes over DON CAMP. from 6 S. Lincs Bn	
MOISLAINS	14--		Regl. Sert Army Commander visits Coys at Training	
"	15--		Coy Training attack practices Musketry &c	
"	16--		On the 21-2-18 Lt Col Neill from B.G.O. re Essex Regt. relinquishes command of Batt. and Lt Col G.B. Hill O.B.E takes over command.	
"	17--			

Army Form C. 2118.

WAR DIARY
or
INTELLIGENCE SUMMARY.

(Erase heading not required.)

Instructions regarding War Diaries and Intelligence Summaries are contained in F. S. Regs., Part II. and the Staff Manual respectively. Title pages will be prepared in manuscript.

Place	Date	Hour	Summary of Events and Information	Remarks and references to Appendices
MOISLAINS	28/8/18	2.50	Batt. moves to HEUDICOURT and takes over the duties of Batt. in Brigade Support, relieving the 16th Bn. Sherwood Foresters. Route. March to D.20.C. thro' 62° stones by Light Railway to HEUDICOURT. Bn. H.Q. and 2 Companies (A.& C.) in huts in HEUDICOURT, 2 companies (B & D) in Railway Embankment 2000 yds further East.	

Mough
Lieut Colonel
Comdg 2d Lincolnshire Regt

62nd Inf.Bde.
21st Div.

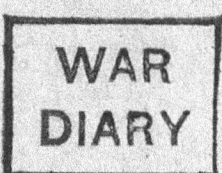

2nd BATTN. THE LINCOLNSHIRE REGIMENT.

M A R C H

1 9 1 8

Attached:-

Appendices.

To.
   D.A.G.
      Base.

Herewith War Dairy of 2nd Bn. Lincolnshire Regt. for period 1st. March 1918 to 31st March 1918.

20.4.18.   R. Bastard   Lt. Col.
     Commanding 2nd Bn; Lincolnshire Regiment.

WAR DIARY or INTELLIGENCE SUMMARY

Army Form C. 2118.

Place	Date	Hour	Summary of Events and Information	Remarks and references to Appendices
HEUDICOURT	19/3 20/3		Batt. in Brigade Support. Work under O.C. Coy. R.E. Inspection and Training.	
	21/3	5.15am	Batt. received orders from BATTLE POSITIONS. "C" Coy comes under orders of O.C. left sector front line (O.C. 1st Lincolnshire Regt.) A, B & D Coys marched independently to their alloted positions in YELLOW LINE. Batt. Head Qrs. marched to B.Q. Cutting. This operation was rendered extremely difficult owing to a thick fog and Enemy heavy Coy establishing themselves in their positions soon after they stopped shelling to shoot until 10am. Disposition: C Coy with 1st Bn Lincolnshire Regt. B Coy in YELLOW LINE with left Coy resting on Railway at Rly Cutting at Y.23.a.8.4. Right Coy at approx Y.18 central. D Coy at Rly Cutting at Y.23 central, and the right. Here positions were maintained all day against repeated attacks by the ENEMY. About 12 Noon a party of the ENEMY succeeded in getting round the left flank under cover of a sunken road at W.18.c.9.3. The party was engaged by Bn. Head Qrs. and a Lewis Team of the Machine Gun Bn. A number were killed and the remainder (about 30) surrendered.	
	22/3		No change until 12 Noon when orders were received to retire on HEUDICOURT. At this hour the Enemy had penetrated the line at EPEHY and were threatening the line of retirement. A and D Coys being heavily engaged, Batt. retained in HEUDICOURT and awaited further orders. About 5.30 remains of the Enemy were closing in on HEUDICOURT from two sides and orders were received to retire on GREEN LINE at GURLU WOOD. Batt. fought a rear guard action with the Enemy until nightfall when action was broken off. The Batt. then marched to its alloted position in the GREEN LINE and became Batt. in support.	
GURLU WOOD	23/3		After quiet night Enemy renewed attack about 8am. Batt. received orders to retire from AIZECOURT-LE-HAUT. About 9.30am Lt. Col. Lloyd was wounded and the command of the Batt. The C.O. Lt. Col. Lloyd was wounded and the command of the Batt. was taken over by Major E.E.F. Baker M.C. During this retirement	

WAR DIARY
or
INTELLIGENCE SUMMARY.

Army Form C. 2118.

(Erase heading not required.)

Place	Date	Hour	Summary of Events and Information	Remarks and references to Appendices
HEUDICOURT	1-3-18		MAP REF SHEETS 57cSE 62c. Batt in Brigade Support. Br HQrs A & C Coys in HEUDICOURT. B & D Coys on Railway Embankment W.23.b.20.05.	
	2-"-		WORK. Digging and wiring of the YELLOW LINE	
	3-"-			
	4-"-			
	5-"-			
HEUDICOURT	6-3-18		Batt relieves 12/13 Bn Northumberland Fus. in Left sub-sector front line.	
	7-"-		Disposition A & C Coys front line. "A" Left sector CHAPEL TRENCH and FIVES TRENCH. "C" Right Sector	
Bn HEADQRS	8-"-		RACKET TRENCH, SKITTLE. B & D Coys in support ALLEY and BIRCHWOOD LOOP	
DUG-OUT at Y18.c.9.5.	10-3-18		Inter-Coy relief. D Coy relieving A Coy in Left sector. B Coy relieving C Coy in Right sector. A & C Coys becoming Right and Left support Coys respectively	
	11-"-		No change	
	12-"-			
	13-"-			
	14-"-			
	15-3-18		Inter Coy relief, A Coy relieving D Coy "C" coy relieving B Coy	
	16-"-		No change	
	17-"-			
	18-3-18		Batt is relieved by 10th Bn Lincolnshire Regt and moves back to Brigade support at HEUDICOURT. {Battln Coy moves to Counter attack coy position at W.23.b.30.05 Embankment and 60 other ranks	
			On the night of 18/19th a party of 2 Officers and belonging to "C" Coy carried out a successful raid on the Enemy Trenches. Officer in command 2nd Lt F.C. Harper R.Warwick Regt (att.). Operation Orders, Narrative re Allotier task	

WAR DIARY or INTELLIGENCE SUMMARY

Army Form C. 2118.

Place	Date	Hour	Summary of Events and Information	Remarks and references to Appendices
GURLU WOOD continued	23/3/18		A line of trenches running parallel to the NURLU-PERONNE ROAD, were manned by the Batn. with Left flank resting on road, west junction of NURLU-MOISLAINS ROADS. The 1st Batn Lincolnshire Regt. continuing the line to the left. This position was maintained until 3 pm, when it became untenable though The Enemy turning the flank. The retirement was continued in extended order, falling back on HAUT-ALLAINES in extended order, when it was taken up by garrison. Practically The whole of The retirement was carried out under hostile M.G fire. A new line was taken up on The high ground to N.W. of HAUT-ALLAINES but this was not maintained for very long, and the Batn moved back to a line approximately midway between CLERY and BOIS-MARRIÈRES. The Enemy became by This time too pressing and after further reorganising The Batn. took up a defensive position for The night. By The night The Batn. had dwindled to 6 officers and about 40 ranks.	
NEAR CLERY	24/3		The night passed without events, but soon after dawn many of The ENEMY advanced to The attack. These were held up by our fire for some time, but our right flank became increasingly dangerous and to prevent envelopment the Batn. had to be withdrawn. By this time The ENEMY had got well round the whole flank and was bringing fire to bear from our right rear. From this time onwards the fighting consisted of a series of delaying actions, the line of retirement being in the direction of HEM which was traced about 11 am. Casualties had been ever and only 4 officers and 19 O. Ranks (including Stragglers from other units) remained. The positions now held by early Ammunition for this batn (Batn. of the 35th Division told in the high ground astride the HEM-CLERY road). About 6 pm orders of The 2/1st DW were withdrawn and ordered to march back to MARICOURT and from thence to SUZANNE where the night was passed.	

Army Form C. 2118.

WAR DIARY
or
INTELLIGENCE SUMMARY.
(Erase heading not required.)

Instructions regarding War Diaries and Intelligence Summaries are contained in F. S. Regs., Part II. and the Staff Manual respectively. Title pages will be prepared in manuscript.

Place	Date	Hour	Summary of Events and Information	Remarks and references to Appendices
SUZANNE	25/3/18		Batt. marched to BRAY. A number of Officers NCO's & men rejoining Batt. at this place, the party comprised of which and the bank from leave, also school of instruction, also a number Base Depot sufficient to bring the Batt. during the retirement, a composite Coy of 300 rifles and 100 others was formed under Lt. A. Holliday and marched to BRAY on a composite Batt. formed by 62nd Inf Bde. when the command of the Coy found devolved on Lt. Holliday daily rejoined the Batt. on 30th.	
CHIPILLY	26/3/18		Batt H.Qrs. and remainder of Batt. marched at 10pm en route to CHIPILLY where the night was spent. Holden and left all ranks with exception of those of Hd Qr. Staff formed into the 4 form part of composite Coy found left of 7th Inf Bde. Batt. to form into to BRESLE.	
BRESLE	27/3/18		At 10am remaining units Batt. form part of composite Coy. (under command of Major Clare) attacked from Coy. 62nd Inf Bde. under The Coy marched to BAZIEUX and took up a position (4pr) The Coy marched to BAZIEUX and took up a defensive position, where it remained until 8 pm. At 8pm it was relieved by the 3rd Australian Division, after which it marched to BEAUCOURT arriving by all ranks from the composite coys. a party of all arms.	
BEAUCOURT	28/3/18		Reorganisation and rest.	
"	29/3/18		Batt. marched to BONNAY to form part of Brigade in support of 10th Australian Inf. Bde.	
BONNAY	30/3/18		Batt. marched to POULAINVILLE. The remainder of the Batt. at this place, coy under Lieut. E.R. Holliday rejoining the Batt. at this place.	
POULAINVILLE	31/3/18		Batt. embussed at 3·15pm and proceeded to HANGEST where the Battn. is found in billets.	

A P P E N D I C E S .

SECRET.   Copy No ___9___

62nd Infantry Brigade Order No. 74.

Ref. Map
57C. S.E. 1/20,000.   17th March 1918.

1. 'C' Coy. 2nd Lincolnshire Regt. will carry out a raid on Strong Point in BEET TRENCH.

   Objective.   X.8.c.78.82 - X.8.a.69.04 and Sap
                X.8.a.68.03 to X.8.a.60.00.
                X.8.c.88.89 - X.8.a.71.04.

2. The objects of the raid are :-
   1. To obtain an identification.
   2. To kill Germans.

3. Zero hour will be 1 a.m. 18.3.18.

4. Total strength of raiding party will be 2 Officers and 60 O.R. 2nd Lieut. F.O.HARPER will be in command. The party will be divided into

   (a) Covering Party. - 1 Sergt. and 20 O.R. (including one Lewis Gun Section).

   (b) Attacking Party. - 2 Officers and 40 O.R.

   Both parties will leave our lines at the North end of RACKET TRENCH at X.7.d.45.10 and will proceed to the track junction at X.7.d.96.49.
   The covering party will leave the track junction at Zero minus 90 minutes, and will take up a position on the flanks of the Assembly position. The attacking party will leave the track junction at Zero minus 50 minutes, and will assemble North of the track leading to BEET TRENCH at X.8.c.90.90 on a line X.8.c.46.76 - X.8.a.40.02, 180 yards from objective. All arrangements must be completed by Zero minus 15 minutes.

5. Artillery arrangements.

   (1) From Zero to Zero plus 4.   There will be a hurricane bombardment from X.8.d.22.41 along BEET TRENCH to X.8.a.48.43, being especially intense on the objective and sap. This will be carried out by 18 pdrs.

(2) **From Zero to Zero plus 40.**   There will be a curtain bombardment along the line of the light railway from X.8.d.63.82 to X.8.a.62.60 by 18 pdrs., from X.8.d.44.56 to X.8.b.63.13 and on the cross roads X.8.b.34.42 by 4.5 Hows. Along GUISLAINS TRENCH from X.8.b.63.23 to X.8.b.33.69 by 6 in. Hows.

(3) **At Zero plus 4.**   The 18 pdr. barrage between X.8.d.10.66 and X.8.a.55.29 will lift to thicken the curtain on the light railway mentioned above.

(4) The barrage will cease at Zero plus 40 mins.

6. At Zero the attacking party will move up as close to the barrage as possible, and at Zero plus 4 mins. will rush the objective.

The attacking party will be divided into 4 sections,

No. 1 Section will rush trench end at X.8.c.76.82.
No. 2 Section   :   :   :   at X.8.c.70.95.
No. 3 Section   :   :   the sap at X.8.a.80.00.
No. 4 Section   :   enter the Support trench at X.8.a.75.03 and will move down the trench towards the Sunken Road running through X.8.b and c. 4 men will be specially detailed to get on the top of the trench and move in the open. Blocks will be established on the flanks and at trench junctions. The role of this party will be to clear the Support trench of any enemy.

7. Detailed orders as regards formations, action on reaching objective, and withdrawal will be issued by O.C. Raiding party. Every officer, N.C.O and man must be thoroughly acquainted with his role.

8. At Zero plus 20, attacking party will withdraw. Signal for the withdrawal will be given by O.C. Attacking party and will be a long blast on the syren whistle, which will be repeated by all Officers and N.C.Os. Covering party will not withdraw till attacking party has passed through it.

9. From Zero plus 20 Very lights (white) will be fired from Railway Embankment X.13.a.20.40, at intervals of one minute to give the party their direction in the withdrawal. Brigade Intelligence Officer will make necessary arrangements.

10.   Prisoners and identity discs and all papers taken from the dead will be sent immediately to Bde. H.Q., and the number of their regiment will be wired at the earliest possible moment. This information may be vital. Brigade Intelligence Officer will make necessary arrangements.

11.   A proportion of wirecutters and electric torches will be carried.

12.   One or two men will be specially detailed for collecting in a sandbag, papers and identity discs from the dead.

13.   No letters or other documents or marks of identification will be carried by the raiding party.

14.   Special raiding identity discs will be issued to all ranks in the Raiding party.

15.   O.C. Raiding Party will send a written report to Bde. H.Q. by 9 a.m. on the morning following the raid.

16.   In view of possible retaliation O.C. Right and Left Battns. will make arrangements to evacuate during the raid such portions of the front system as they consider necessary. Trenches evacuated must be re-occupied as soon as possible.

17.   O.C. Raiding party and an officer from each Artillery Brigade will report at Bde. H.Q. to synchronise watches at 8 p.m. tonight.

18.   Acknowledge.

R E Hobson
Lieut.
A/Bde. Major,
62 Infantry Bde.

Issued through Signals
at 1.30 p.m.

Copy No. 1 & 2 - War Diary & File.
        3 - G.O.C.
        4 - Staff Captain.
        5 - Intell. Officer.
        6 - Signal
        7 - 12/13 Northd Fus.
        8 - 1 Lincoln R.
        9 - 2 Lincoln R.
       10 - 62 T.M.Bty.
       11 - 21 Division.
       12 - C.R.A.

Copy No. 13 - D.H.G.O.
       14 - 108 Bde. R.F.A.
       15 - 95 " "
       16 - 150 " "
       17 - 64 Inf. Bde.
       18 - 110 " "
       19 - S.A. " "
       20 - 97 F. Co. R.E.
       21 - 126 F.Co. R.E.
       22 - 6" Bty. (C.O. 21 D.A.)
       23 - O.C. Raiding party.

SECRET.   B.M. 68/77.

1. The Raid on the Strong Point in BEET TRENCH will be carried out tonight (18/19th), and all details (except Zero hour) will be the same as in 62nd Inf. Bde. Order No. 74, forwarded yesterday.

2. Zero hour will be 3.0 a.m. 19.3.18.

3. O.C. Raiding Party and an officer from each Artillery Bde. will report to Bde. H.Q. to synchronise watches at 8 p.m. tonight.

4. A c k n o w l e d g e. ✓

R.C. Hobson
Lieut,
A/Bde. Major,
62nd Infantry Bde.

18.3.18.

Copy to all recipients of Bde. Order No. 74.

Report on Raid carried out by
C.Company 2nd Bn Lincolnshire Regt
on night 18/19th March 1918.

1. **Object.**
   (a) To obtain an identification.
   (b) To kill Germans.

2. **Objective.**
   Strong Point in BEET TRENCH. X.8.c.78.82 - X.8.a.69.04.
   and Sap X.8.a.68.93 to X.8.a.60.00.   X.8.c.88.89 -
   X.8.a.71.04.

3. **Strength.**
   2 Officers and 60 Other Ranks divided into
   (a) Attacking party - 2 Officers and 40 O.R.
   (b) Covering Party - 1 Sergt and 20 O.R (including 1 L.G.Section).
   2Lt F.C.Harper was in command.

4. **Plan.**
   (a) Reconnaissance and Air Photographs showed that the trench
   X.8.c.78.82 - X.8.a.69.04 had a post at the Southern end and
   that the trench was provided with shelters, that the sap was
   occupied, and that BEET TRENCH had a traffic path running
   behind it denoting that it was either held as a defensive
   position or used for accommodation of garrison.
   The attacking party was divided into four columns of equal
   strength, 3 columns to deal with front trench sap and 1 column
   to go through to BEET TRENCH just South of sap and then move
   South along BEET TRENCH to deal either with defensive garrison,
   dugouts and any enemy coming back from front trench.
   (b) The covering party took up a position on a line X.8.c.45.75 -
   X.8.a.40.03, 180 yards from objective - Attacking party also
   formed up on this line.

5. **NARRATIVE.**
   At 1.45 a.m the covering and attacking parties left our line at
   North end of RACKET TRENCH at X.7.d.45.10. and proceeded to the
   track junction at X.7.d.95.48. From here the covering party moved
   to take up its position.
   The attacking party followed at 2.10 a.m and assembled on the
   line taken up by the covering party. All arrangements were
   complete at 2.45 a.m.
   Everything was perfectly quiet while the parties were forming up
   on their assembly position, the moon had gone down but there was
   sufficient light to verify that the columns were in their correct
   positions.
   At 3 a.m a hurricane bombardment started and the attacking party
   moved forward to the edge of the barrage.
   At 3.4 a.m the barrage lifted and the strong point was rushed.
   No 1 column entered the trench close to read at X.8.c.72.82.
   As this column had to use wire-cutters there was a slight delay
   before the party could enter the trench. This part of the trench
   was garrisoned by 2 machine gunners and a machine gun, both the
   gunners were killed and the machine gun was blown up with 2 bombs.
   One officer and 5 men were brought out of a dugout. The Officer
   and one man were killed and the remainder surrendered.
   No 2 Column entered the trench at X.8.c.70.95. The wire here had
   been well cut and the party was therefore able to rush the trench
   as the barrage lifted.   This column took one prisoner,
   bayoneted or bombed five of the enemy and also bombed 1 dugout.
   No 3 column had to move to its left in going forward to avoid
   some wire and before reaching BEET TRENCH a brilliant ground flare
   lighted well in rear of BEET TRENCH disclosed a party of 7 of
   the enemy moving forward over the open from the left front.
   This party was met and all killed.   On the party moving down
   BEET TRENCH 6 of the enemy were seen and killed. A dugout in
   BEET TRENCH was found to be empty.
   This column sustained 2 casualties owing to a badly thrown bomb.

(2)

No 4 Column entered the Sap at X.8.c.60.00. The wire here was very well cut. The Sap was found to be empty but a German was encountered at the Eastern end of the Sap was killed. On reaching BEET TRENCH the column moved up it to the left where an empty dugout was found, a block was formed here. A party of Germans were seen moving across the open in the direction of the Block, 2 men of this party were killed and 1 was seen to escape.

General Remarks.

The trenches were badly damaged by shell fire.
Dugouts were merely splinter proof and afforded very little protection.
Hostile trench mortars were fired from both flanks and bombs, and rifle fire came from the North.
The two counter-attacks over the open also came from a Northerly direction.
Two brilliant ground flares were lighted during the raid well behind BEET TRENCH.
Our revolvers were most useful in meeting the sudden and unexpected situation and were used with good effect against the counterattacks. In two instances bomb throwers became detached from their bomb carriers.
The time for our barrage on the strong point was exactly correct and our men were able to move close up to it before it lifted.
The shooting of our gunners was extremely accurate and gained the admiration of all men of the party.
Considering the immense difficulty of observation during the previous wire cutting, the results of the wire cutting Battery were exceptionally good. There was but little hostile artillery retaliation, this fell chiefly in the Valley X.7.d.5.2.
At 3.20 a.m the signal for the withdrawal was given and the column withdrew in an orderly manner to the shelters at X.7.d.9.2.
The party then returned to our own lines.
The excellence of the Artillery fire and the dash, spirit and determination of our men insured the success of this operation.

6. **Our Casualties.**
   Wounded.   1 Officer.   6 Other Ranks.
   Missing.   1 Other Rank.

   Enemy Casualties.
   Killed 23 (not including those in dugouts which were bombed)
   Prisoners 5 (including 1 wounded).

7. Decorations awarded
   2nd/Lt F.C. Harper Military Cross
   116044 A/Cpl F. Barker D.C.M. 200565 L/Sgt A. Osborne M.M.
   1178 Cpl S. Vicker M.M. 4163? Pte W. Tures M.M.
   17440 Pte J. Hardy M.M. 242194 Pte J. Leary M.M.
   38941 " J. Deeks M.M.

   Lloyd
   Lieut Colonel.
   Comdg. and Lincolnshire Regiment.

2nd Bn Lincolnshire Regiment.

List of Casualties From 21.3.18 to 2.4.18.

OFFICERS.

2/Lt F.L. Osborne	D. Of Wounds	21.3.18.
Capt S. Wilson	Wounded	23.3.18
Capt Rev M. Tron D.S.O. M.C.	Wounded (at Duty) still	21.3.18
2/Lt A.R. Hill (Royal Warwick Regt attached 2nd Lincs)	Wounded	22.3.18
2/Lt W.F. Hyde	do	21.3.18
2/Lt G. Molyneux	do	23.3.18
2/Lt V.G.B. Watkins	do	21.3.18
2/Lt H.T. Richardson	do	21.3.18
2/Lt L. Caldicott	do	24.3.18
2/Lt A.E. Watson	do	26.3.18
Capt J.M. Lockie (12/13th N. Fus attd 2nd Lincs)	Wounded & Missing	22.3.18
2/Lt C.F. Willcox (Royal Warwick Regt attached 2nd Lincs)	Missing	22.3.18
2/Lt F.G. Cole	do	21.3.18
2/Lt B. Nightingale	do	22.3.18
2/Lt R.H. Stafford	do	23.3.18
Lt Col E.P. Lloyd	Wounded	
Lt & Qr Mr W. Collins (Royal Warwick Regt attached 2nd Lincs)	Wounded	26.3.18.

Other Ranks.

Killed	Wounded	Wounded & Missing	Missing	Total
31	95	9	238	373

19.4.18.

R Bastard Lt Col
Commdg 2nd Bn Lincolnshire Regiment.

62nd Brigade.

21st Division.

2nd BATTALION

LINCOLNSHIRE REGIMENT

APRIL 1918.

WAR DIARY or INTELLIGENCE SUMMARY

Army Form C. 2118.

2nd Warwickshire Regt

Place	Date	Hour	Summary of Events and Information	Remarks and references to Appendices
HANGEST	1/4/18		Battalion entrains at HANGEST STATION en route to PESCHENDER	
PESCHNOEK	2		Both detrain at PESCHOEK and proceed by motor lorry to KEMMEL	
KEMMEL	3		Both resting and reorganising	
KEMMEL	4		The Battn relieve the 8th Bn 8th Northumberland Fus in front line trenches near WYTSCHAETE. South of the main PRINCE RUPERTS DUG-OUT. Disposition of Bn from Lt to Right B Coy from Lt to B Dugout C & D Coys front line. (O.10.1.R.3.Ch/18)	
WYTSCHAETE	5		D 2 Coys from lt to M Cross.	
			The Battn is relieved by 9th N. F. P. W. Fus and moves into KEMMEL SHELTERS Camp. (N.6.6.3.)	
KEMMEL SHELTERS			Cleaning up and fitting out 1½ company officers of the 8th Batts join under Major E.H.F. Bates M.C.	
	8.9		Bn was ordered to proceed to FORESTERS CAMP (H.10.a.6.6)	
	10		An enemy attack was made on the Lt. Bde front, the Bn was ordered to occupy a Coy in PICKET FARM line in line of WYTSCHAETE. (A detailed account of Hostibutin is attached hereto)	

Army Form C. 2118.

WAR DIARY
or
INTELLIGENCE SUMMARY.
(Erase heading not required.)

Instructions regarding War Diaries and Intelligence Summaries are contained in F. S. Regs. Part II. and the Staff Manual respectively. Title pages will be prepared in manuscript.

Place	Date	Hour	Summary of Events and Information	Remarks and references to Appendices
WYTSCHAETE	11/13		In front line trenches near WYTSCHAETE. Batt. was gassed with M.G. 12 (an attack imminent)	
	12/13		Batt. relieved by 18/13 Bn H'lers and marched to camp at	
	13		ROSSIGNOL WOOD 17/8 a.e.2.	
	14		12 noon Batt. moved to a position near LAICHE FARM 1/28 a.m. B at 4.30 p.m. the Batt. carried out a counter attack on El PECKHAM	
			MAEDELSTEDE Line (an attack movement)	
	15		In front line Batt. to relieve 14 (?) Composite Bn 3.P.0.m	
	16		and march to SIEGE FARM Nh. C. 26. Resting	
SIEGE FARM	17/18		Batt. marched to SCOTTISH CAMP G.21.b.6.i near OUDERDOM	
SCOTTISH CAMP	19		Reorganisation Coy Training Specialist Training	
	20		Batt. moved to a position in reserve near DICKEBUSCH	
	21		Battalion quiet at H.26.c.6.b.	
NEAR DICKEBUSCH	28		No change	
	29		Batt. moved to Ouderdom position in relief of R. Composite	

Army Form C. 2118.

WAR DIARY
or
INTELLIGENCE SUMMARY.
(Erase heading not required.)

Instructions regarding War Diaries and Intelligence Summaries are contained in F. S. Regs. Part II. and the Staff Manual respectively. Title pages will be prepared in manuscript.

Place	Date	Hour	Summary of Events and Information	Remarks and references to Appendices
Kem-DICKEBUSCH	29th		Battalion(2nd)Bn Distribution Batt in line from RIDGE WOOD to SCOTTISH WOOD. Batt. Hd Qrs Gr. Hyams	
	30th		Battn relieved by 1st Bn Yorks Regt and march to Villets aux (Cugno) GHQ b Enclose	
			For casualties during period 1st to 30th April 1916 see attached list	

R Bastard Lieut Col
Commanding 2nd Bn Lincolnshire Regt

2nd Bn Lincolnshire Regiment.
.........oOo..........

List of Casualties

OFFICERS.

2/Lieut G. Shaw	Killed in Action	12.4.18.
2/Lieut R.R. Wilcockson	Wounded in Action	11.4.18.
Capt R.B. Pritchard M.C. (14th North Fus att 2nd Lincs Regt) Wounded		16.4.18.
Capt J.H.G. Lillywhite	Wounded in Action	16.4.18.
2/Lt L.W. Pacy (3rd Royal Warwick Regt att 2nd Lincoln Regt) Wounded in Action		25.4.18.
2/Lt H.V. Joyce	do do	27.4.18.
2/Lt E.V. Leach do do	do (Gassed)	29.4.18
2/Lt G.W. Hodge	Missing	27.4.18.

....

Other Ranks.

Killed	Wounded	(Wounded Gassed)	Missing	Total
22	210	9	52	293.

2nd Lincolnshire Regiment.

Account of Operations from 10th April to 19th April 1918.

On night of April 10th?

2nd Lincolnshire Regt. received orders to march and occupy a gap in the line from ONRAET WOOD to STANYZER CABARET, the 12/13th Northumberland Fusiliers filling up the gap further South.

When proceeding down the VIERSTRAAT - WYTSCHAETE Road, the advanced guards came in touch with the Black Watch at GRAND BOIS, after which point no troops were met, but abandoned guns were pulled across the road.

The battalion made good the road from ONRAET WOOD to STANYZER CABARET, and at about 4.30 a.m. on the 11th got in touch with the Black Watch on our left at ONRAET WOOD, and the 12/13th Northumberland Fusiliers on the right; a few enemy patrols were met with on the right, and shots exchanged; the road we were on was then subjected to a heavy barrage. At 5.30 a.m. according to orders, 2nd Lincolnshire Regiment advanced and occupied the Corps Line of Posts from SOMER FARM to STANYZER CABARET.

During the advance and during the day the Battalion captured 14 prisoners from 4th, 393rd and 76th Regiments, and killed a good lot more by Lewis Gun and rifle fire.

The advance was carried out during a very dark night, at very short notice and over ground which was only known to a very few people in the battalion, and was carried out up to time without a hitch. The Battalion remained in this line till relieved on the night of 15/16th, during which time the position was repeatedly very heavily shelled, and numerous casualties were inflicted on the enemy by Lewis Gun and rifle fire, and touch well maintained with the enemy by patrols.

After relief on the morning of the 16th the Battalion marched back to Camp at ROSSIGNOL WOOD, which they reached at 4 a.m., and stood to and reconnoitred the VIERSTRAAT KEMMEL ROAD trenches. An hour after standing down orders were received to man the trenches, and soon afterwards to advance with No. 2 Composite Battalion, 39th Division, and attack and capture the PECKHAM - MAEDELSTEDE FARM ridge. The attack was cancelled and the 2 battalions then occupied a line running through LAGACHE FARM and VANDAMME FARM.

Orders were received at 4 p.m. to counter-attack at 6.0 p.m. 1st Objective - the PECKHAM - MAEDELSTEDE Line. 2nd Objective - the old line at WYTSCHAETE. The time for attack was afterwards changed to 7.30 p.m. and was to be in conjunction with the French on the right and the Seaforths on the left. The attack was most gallantly carried out under very heavy M.G. fire from the front and right flank, and pushed to a trench within 50 to 100 yards of the 1st objective, which was made good. This attack was carried out by the Battalion after a week's heavy fighting, no sleep the previous night, and only partially reorganised after the recent SOMME fighting. It was carried out with the greatest dash and vigour, and only the fine spirit of all ranks in the face of every difficulty (such as heavy enfilade fire from the right, where the French attack never developed) enabled the attack to gain the ground it did. The Battalion consolidated the ground won, with the No. 2 Composite Battalion on their left.

'A' Coy. 12/13th Northd Fus. was attached to the Battn. took part in the attack, and behaved splendidly. The Battalion was relieved on night 17/18th.

Brigadier General,
Comdg. 62nd Infantry Bde.

2nd BATTALION LINCOLNSHIRE REGIMENT.

W A R   D I A R Y.

Period.

1st MAY 1918.   to   31st MAY 1918.

Army Form C. 2118.

WAR DIARY
or
INTELLIGENCE SUMMARY.
(Erase heading not required.)

Instructions regarding War Diaries and Intelligence Summaries are contained in F. S. Regs., Part II. and the Staff Manual respectively. Title pages will be prepared in manuscript.

Place	Date	Hour	Summary of Events and Information	Remarks and references to Appendices
CAMP.D.14 BUSSEBOOM	1st	6p	Ref Map Sheet 51 HAZEBROUCK, Sheet 28 HAVRE, Belgium, SOISSONS 1/100,000	
BEAUVOORDE	2nd		Batn Marches to Billets in BEAUVOORDE	
LEDERZEELE	3rd		Batn Marches to Camp nr LEDERZEELE	
"	4th		Batn resting cleaning up	
"	5th		and reorganising	
"	6th		Batn Marches to ARQUES and entrains about 2.15am 6th	
In Train	7th		In Train	
LHERY	8th 9th 10th 11th		Batn detrained at SAVIGNY and marches to camp LHERY In Camp at LHERY Work Coy Training Specialist Training and Range Practice	
LHERY	12th		Batn marches to VAUX-VARENNES AREA and moves into camp Nr BOUVANCOURT	
1st BOUVANCOURT	13th		Batn marches to position in Brigade Reserve and take over camp from the 41st Batn of CHASSEURS-A-PIED near CHALONS LE-VERGEUR	
CAMP H CHALONS LE VERGEUR	14th to 20th		Batn in Brigade Reserve. Work Coy Training Specialist Training etc.	

Army Form C. 2118.

WAR DIARY
or
INTELLIGENCE SUMMARY.
(Erase heading not required.)

Instructions regarding War Diaries and Intelligence Summaries are contained in F. S. Regs., Part II. and the Staff Manual respectively. Title pages will be prepared in manuscript.

Place	Date	Hour	Summary of Events and Information	Remarks and references to Appendices
CHALONS-LE-VERGUER	21/9		Lt. Coln relieves 1st Bn Lincolnshire Regt in front line trenches from SAPIGNIEL. Nucleus fairly under the command of Major Labette receiving in camp at CHALONS-LE-VERGUER.	
FRONT LINE TRENCHES	22/9 23/9		In front line trenches.	
	24/9	7.10am	The enemy opened a heavy bombardment of line and other gun active continued until about 11am. At this hour under a thick smoke screen the enemy attacked, and apparently broke through the line to the R. of the sector held by the Battn, who seem to have been almost immediately surrounded. Two officers and about 30 other Ranks only got thro' away the nucleus party and transport moved back to a point about 1/2 mile SE of BOUVANCOURT.	
		10pm	The enemy were repulsed on BOUVANCOURT. Transport continued the retirement. Brigade nucleus parties under command of Major Hunter & Lieut Ashley covering the retirement moved to PEVY.	
PEVY	25/9	6am	A defensive position was taken up on the high ground E. of PROUILLY	

WAR DIARY
or
INTELLIGENCE SUMMARY.

Army Form C. 2118.

(Erase heading not required.)

Place	Date	Hour	Summary of Events and Information	Remarks and references to Appendices
Nr PROUILLY	28th		PROUILLY. This position though heavily attacked was held until the evening when the whole force were ordered to withdraw across the VESLE RIVER. The Batn. nucleus party where then ordered to defend a portion of the river and a line of posts were occupied about 1 mile E. of MUIZON. This line was held until 4.30 pm on the 29th.	
Nr MUIZON	29th		The enemy made repeated attacks during the day but was held off until evening. About 4pm a heavy enemy bombardment commenced. The posts till right when the line gave way on both flanks. The Bn. tactly was almost enveloped before this was discovered, but managed to withdraw under cover of the woods, and after working round to MERY-PREMECY. March continues to VAUCIENNES.	
MERY-PREMECY	30th		to VAUCIENNES.	
VAUCIENNES	31st		Moved continues to SOULIERES.	

(Attacks) Roll of casualties on Form C. 2118/14.

F.J. Robertson Lt Col
1st Bn 3rd Lincolns Reg.

2nd Battalion Lincolnshire Regiment.
LIST OF CASUALTIES.

Rank.	Name	Casualty.
2nd Lt;	R.W.Hartley.	Wounded & Missing 29.5.18.
"	W.E.Deavin.	Wounded 29.5.18.
		Rejoined 2.6.18.
Lt;Col;	R.Bastard.D.S.O.	Missing. 27.5.18.
Captain.	J.T.Preston.	" " "
"	H.Marshall.	" " "
"	G.R.Holliday.M.C.	" " "
Lieut;.	G.Matson.	" " "
2nd.Lt;	F.Donell.	" " "
"	F.Havers.	" " "
"	C.Race.	" " "
"	M.D.Grieve.	" " "
"	V.Nocton.	" " "
"	S.G.Sole.M.C.	" " "
"	A.R.Braddy.	" " "
"	E.L.Jones.	" " "
"	B.W.Pye.	" " "
"	L.J.Turner.	" " "
"	R.W.Osgerby.	" " "
Lieut; M.O.	A.McCormick.R.A.M.C.	" " "
Lieut;.	F.F.Davies.	Wounded (at duty) 29.5.18.

OTHER RANKS.

Killed.	Wounded.	Missing.
6.	53.	327.

5.6.18.

Commanding 2nd Bn; Lincolnshire Regiment

2nd BATTALION LINCOLNSHIRE REGIMENT.

W A R   D I A R Y.

P E R I O D.

1st JUNE 1918 to 30th JUNE 1918.

Army Form C. 2118.

WAR DIARY
or
INTELLIGENCE SUMMARY.
(Erase heading not required.)

Instructions regarding War Diaries and Intelligence Summaries are contained in F. S. Regs. Part II. and the Staff Manual respectively. Title pages will be prepared in manuscript.

Place	Date	Hour	Summary of Events and Information	Remarks and references to Appendices
SOULIERES	1/7/16		Ref. Maps { SOISSONS 1/100,000 / BEAUVAIS / DIEPPE }	
			Bath in billets. 4 Officers and 58 O.Ranks sent to four parts of the 212th Indepdent Brigade. Bath hors de combat small nucleus only	
"	2/7/16		remaining in billets.	
			No change.	
"	3/7/16		Bath proceeded by March Route to VILLEYENARD	
VILLEYENARD	6/7/16		Bath resting and fitting and Lewis gun training.	
	8/7/16		Lieut Col E. O. Moger D.P.O. arrived on the 5/7/16 and takes over	
			command of the Bath from Major F.J. Cohen M.C.	
"	9/7/16		Bath marches to BEAUVAIS	
BEAUVAIS	10/7/16		General training	
	12/7/16			
"	14/7/16		Bath marches to SEZANNE and entrains	
EN ROUTE	15/7/16	10pm	Bath detrains at LONGPRÉ and marches to HALLENCOURT	
HALLENCOURT	16/7/16		Resting	
"	x		Bath marches to AUMÂTRE	

WAR DIARY
or
INTELLIGENCE SUMMARY.
(Erase heading not required.)

Army Form C. 2118.

Place	Date	Hour	Summary of Events and Information	Remarks and references to Appendices
AUMÂTRE	16/6 to 20/6		Specialist training. Bn to be reinforced by a draft of 15 Officers & 514 O.Ranks on the 19th. Draft rejoin Batt. from 2/5th Independent Brigade on the 20th.	
AUMÂTRE	21/6		Batt. marches to BAZINVAL	
BAZINVAL	22/6		Batt. marches to MELLEVILLE	
MELLEVILLE	23/6 to 30/6		Specialist section and Platoon training. Re-organization	
			Casualties during month. Wounded O.Ranks. 1.	

M. Lloyd Lewis Col.
Commanding
2nd Bn Lincolnshire

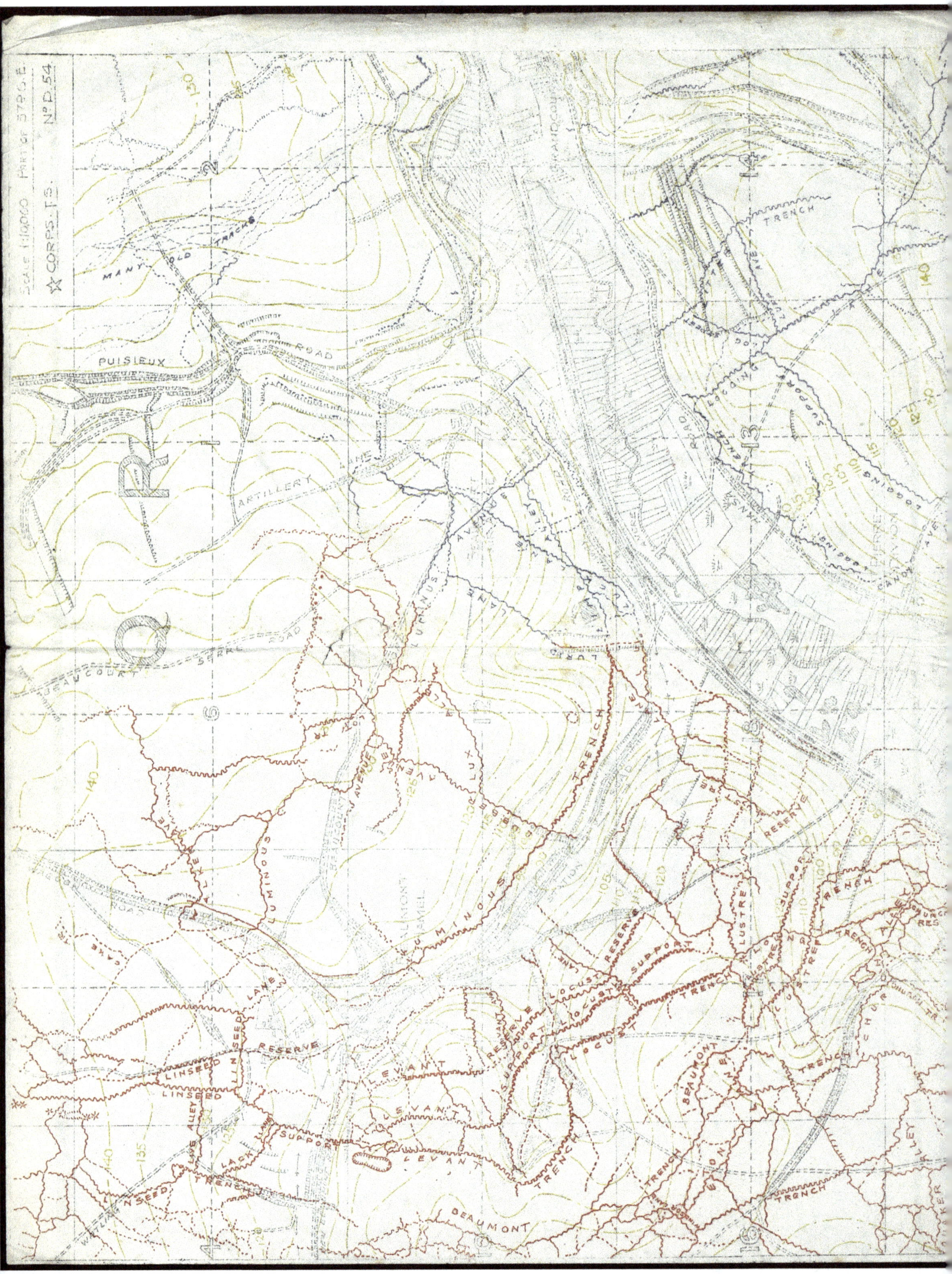
SCALE 1:10,000 PART OF 57D S.E.
CORPS. T.S.
No D.54
MANY OLD TRACKS
PUISIEUX
ROAD
ARTILLERY
BEAUCOURT
SERRE ROAD
LUMINOUS
AVENUE
LURID
LANE
TRENCH
LUX
LINSEED
RESERVE
LEVANT
SUPPORT
LOCUST
LUSTRE
BEAUMONT
ALLEY

2ND BATTALION LINCOLNSHIRE REGT

WAR DIARY

FOR PERIOD

1st to 31st JULY 1918

Army Form. C. 2118.

WAR DIARY
or
INTELLIGENCE SUMMARY.
(Erase heading not required.)

Ref Maps SHEET Dieppe 57 P 1:40,000

Place	Date	Hour	Summary of Events and Information	Remarks and references to Appendices
MELLEVILLE	1/7/18		Batt. marched to LONGROY - GAMACHES and entrained. Detrained same day at PUCHEVILLERS and marched to billets at BEAUQUESNE	
BEAUQUESNE	2/7/18 to 13/7/18		Company and Specialist Training. Range Practices &c	
"	14/7/18		Batt. moves by march route to TOUTENCOURT, see appendix I attached	
TOUTENCOURT	15 & 16/7/18		Company and Specialist Training. Range Practices &c	
"	17/7/18		Batt. moves by march route to RAINCHEVAL, see appendix II attached	
RAINCHEVAL	18/7/18 to 23/7/18		Company and Specialist Training. Range Practices &c	
"	24/7/18		Batt. moves to position in Brigade Reserve forward area. Appendix III (see)	
NEAR MAILLY-MAILLET	25/7/18		Batt. takes over right sub-sector front line trenches Appendix IV (see)	
	29-31/7/18		No change	

Casualties during month. Wounded 1 Rank

R Lloyd Lieut Col
Commdg. 2nd Batt. Lincolnshire Regt.

Appendix No 1

2nd BATTN LINCOLNSHIRE REGIMENT.

OPERATION ORDER No. 42.

S E C R E T.   Copy No. 2

Ref. Map Sheet 57d. 1/20,000.

1. The Battalion will move to TOUTENCOURT (8 Kilometres) this afternoon. Route - BEAUQUESNES - PUCHEVILLERS - TOUTENCOURT.

2. The Battalion will parade in Column of Route facing South at 2.15 p.m. Head of Column at North end of Square, BEAUQUESNES. Order of march - Battn H.Q., "C", "D", "A", "B" Companies.
   On marching off, 100 yards distance will be maintained between companies.

3. The strictest march discipline will be maintained.

4. Administrative Orders for above issued separately.

5. Acknowledge.

                                        Capt. & A/Adjt.
                                        2nd Bn Lincolnshire Regiment.
14.7.18.

Copy No.		Copy No.	
1	Office	6	"A" Coy.
2	War Diary	7	"B" Coy.
3	62nd Inf. Bde.	8	"C" Coy.
4	Quartermaster.	9	"D" Coy.
5	Transport Offr.	10	Spare.

APPENDIX No II

SECRET.

2nd BATTN LINCOLNSHIRE REGT.

Copy No. 2

Battn Operation Order No. 43.

Ref. Map Sheet 57d. 1/40,000.

1. The Battalion will move to RAINNEVAL by march route this evening.

2. The Battalion will form up in Column of Route facing North East at 7.25 p.m. Head of column at Road Junction U.1.b.4.3.
Order of March – Bn H.Q., A, B, C, D Companies.
Drums will march at the head of C Company.
After marching off, 100 yards distance will be maintained between companies.

3. Pack animals will march in rear of their respective companies.

4. Administrative Instructions for above move are issued separately.

[signature]
Capt. & A/Adjt.
2nd Bn Lincolnshire Regiment.

18.7.18.

Copy No. 1 Office.
2 War Diary.
3 H.Q., 62nd Bde.
4 Quartermaster.
5 Transport Officer.
6 A Company.
7 B Company.
8 C Company.
9 D Company.
10 R.S.M.
11 Spare.

APPENDIX No. III

SECRET.   Copy No. 2

2nd Battn LINCOLNSHIRE REGIMENT.
OPERATION ORDER No. 44.

Ref Map - Sheet 57d. 1/40,000.   July 24, 1918.

1. The Battalion will relieve the 2nd Battn Royal Irish Regiment (Reserve Battn) in the Mailly Sector to-night, 24th instant.

2. An Advance Party as under will parade at Battn H.Q. at 2 p.m.
   2/Lieut W.E. Deavin and 1 N.C.O. from Bn H.Q.
   1 Officer and 1 N.C.O. per company.
   1 N.C.O. per Platoon.

   This party will be met by Guides at P.12.Central at 4.30 p.m.

3. The Battalion will form up in Column of Route ready to move off at 6.25 p.m. Head of Column at cross-roads, N.12.c.50.69. Order of March - H.Q., "D", "A", "B", "C" Companies. Guides will be met at P.12.Central.
   Lewis Gun limbers will follow in rear of leading Platoon of each company.

4. After marching off, 100 yards will be maintained between companies, WEST of ACHEUX, and 200 yards between Platoons, EAST of ACHEUX.

5. All Defence Schemes, Trench Stores, details of work in hand, etc, will be taken over by companies, and receipts forwarded to Battn H.Q. by 12 noon, 25th instant.

6. Completion of Relief will be reported to Battn H.Q. by Code Word "DELIGHTED".

7. Administrative Instructions are issued separately.

8. ACKNOWLEDGE.

                                        Capt. & A/Adjt.
                                        2nd Bn Lincolnshire Regiment.

DISTRIBUTION.

    Copy No. 1   Office.
            2   War Diary.
            3   62nd Infantry Brigade.
            4   Transport Officer.
            5   Quartermaster.
            6   Regtl Sergeant Major.
            7   O.C., A Coy.
            8   "   B Coy.
            9   "   C Coy.
           10   "   D Coy.
           11   Spare.

2nd Bn Lincolnshire Regiment

APPENDIX No. IV

Operation Order No. 45   Copy No. 2

Ref Map Sheet 57d SE   28th July 1916

1. The 2nd Bn Lincolnshire Regt will relieve elements of 12/13th Bn N. Fus. and 1st Bn Lincolnshire Regiment in the Front line tonight.

2. The Battn will take over positions as given in Preliminary Operation Order.
    D Coy 2nd Bn Lincolnshire Regt will relieve B Coy (Left) & A Coy (Right) 12/13th Bn N Fus.
    B Coy 2nd Bn Lincolnshire Regt will relieve C Coy 1st Bn Lincolnshire Regt.
    C Coy 2nd Bn Lincolnshire Regt will relieve B Coy 1st Bn Lincolnshire Regt.
    A Coy will move to the position allotted to them in P.12.c. under arrangement to be made by O.C. Coys.
    Bn Headquarters & R A Post will remain in their present positions.

3. D Coy leading Platoon will pass W end of BUFFS AVENUE (Q.8.d.55.40) at 10 pm.
    B Coy at 10.15 pm and C Coy at 10.30 pm all movement to be by Platoons.

4. B, C, & D Coys will send guides to Bn Hd Qrs on a scale of 1 per Coy Hd Qrs & 1 per Platoon at 8.30 pm to take back guides of 12/13th N. Fus & 1st Bn Lincolnshire Regt.

5. O.C. Coys will be responsible for guiding their Coys to W end of BUFFS AVENUE.

6. O.C. A Coy will send 1 guide from Coy Hd Qrs & 1 guide per Platoon to report to Hd Qrs 1st Bn Lincolnshire Regt at 11 pm.

7. Relief complete will be reported by code word EGG.

8. Acknowledge.

J. I. Clugs
Capt. & Adjt.
2nd Battn. Lincolnshire Regt.

P.T.O

Distribution

Copy No	
1.	Office
2.	War Diary
3.	Hdqrs. 62nd Inf Bde
4.	12/13th N. Fus.
5.	1st Bn Lincolnshire Regt
6.	Q.M. & T.O
7	A Coy
8	B Coy
9	C Coy
10	D Coy

Confidential.

WAR DIARY.
of the
2nd Bn Lincolnshire Regiment.

from — 1st August 1918
to — 31st August 1918.

WAR DIARY
INTELLIGENCE SUMMARY.
(Erase heading not required.)

Army Form C. 2118.

Place	Date	Hour	Summary of Events and Information	Remarks and references to Appendices
			AUGUST - 1916.	Ref. MAPS.
MAILLY MAILLET	1st		Very quiet during the day. "B" Company holding front line, one platoon BEAUMONT Trench at head of EUFFS AVENUE, Q.10.d.2.7. - Q.10.b.3.4., three platoons in BEAUMONT Reserve 400 yards in rear. "B" and "C" Companies holding localities 400 yards behind BEAUMONT Reserve "B" on left, "C" on right. "A" Company (under 12/13th Northumberland Fusiliers) moved to ACHEUX	Part of 57d S.M. 1/10,000. 57d S.E. 1/20,000. 57c S.W. 1/20,000.
		11.20 p.m.	on account of having been heavily gas shelled. "D" Company in trench on East side of MAILLY MAILLET. Battn Headquarters in vicinity of Bn H.Q. Hostile planes dropped bombs in vicinity of Bn H.Q. during the night.	
	2nd		Active patrolling was carried out, in order to find out exactly how enemy held his front line, with a view to a raid.	
		10 p.m.	Enemy Trench Mortars active during the night on BEAUMONT Trench.	
	3rd	3.30 a.m.	Enemy put down heavy barrage on area of Battalion on our left; a few shells only fell in our area.	
		9 p.m.	"C" and "D" Companies changed over positions. Our patrols were active and found LEVANT Trench held by posts at Q.10.d.5.6., Q.10.b.8.2. and Q.10.b.8./. Patrol was able to get quite close to post at Q.10.b.8.2., when they were bombed.	
	4th	7.30 p.m.	Enemy opened a heavy barrage on front company over which lasted until 8.45 p.m., otherwise nothing unusual to report. "A" Company took "D" Company went to ACHEUX to prepare for raid. "A" Company took over position vacated by "D" Company.	
	5th		Very quiet. Enemy activity below normal.	
	6th	9 p.m.	"B" Company relieved "C" Company in front line. On relief, "C" Company took over position vacated by "B" Company.	

WAR DIARY
or
INTELLIGENCE SUMMARY.
(Erase heading not required.)

Army Form C. 2118.

Instructions regarding War Diaries and Intelligence Summaries are contained in F. S. Regs., Part II. and the Staff Manual respectively. Title pages will be prepared in manuscript.

Place	Date	Hour	Summary of Events and Information	Remarks and references to Appendices
line in BEAUMONT Trench	7th	11 p.m. to 3 a.m.	Enemy heavily shelled with artillery and Trench Mortars our front line in BEAUMONT Trench	
		8 p.m.	"D" Company moved from ACHEUX to MAILLY MAILLET in motor lorries preparatory to carrying out a raid on LEVANT Trench, North and South of Sap at G.10.d.5.6. and down RYL Ravine.	
		11 p.m.	"D" Company formed up on tape line 50 yards East of BEAUMONT Trench and opposite their objective in four parties. Right party to enter LEVANT Trench South of sap and work down trench towards LOCUST Trench as far as G.10.d.8.4. Two centre parties - one party to rush sap, enter and occupy LEVANT Trench at West end of sap, the other party to make through and work down RYL Ravine to Q.10.c.6.b. Left party to enter LEVANT Trench North of sap, leaving one section there, the remaining two sections to move across to LEVANT Support at Q.11.d.1.8. Each party strength one platoon. In addition, 2 Lewis Gun Sections, one on either flank, acted as covering parties in NO MAN'S LAND on flanks of forming up line.	
		12 midnight	Artillery opened a barrage. A standing box barrage was put down on the line, Q.10.b.8.2 - Q.11.a.6.1 - Q.11.c.6.6. A creeping barrage came down on LEVANT Trench and on Q.10.b.6.2 - Q.11.c.1.4. The creeping barrage moved forward at the rate of 100 yards in four minutes, and, on reaching line of standing barrage, became stationary. Machine Guns and Trench Mortars assisted on the flanks. As the barrage opened the raiding parties moved forward up to the barrage, and entered the trench as it lifted. All the parties reached their objectives but did not encounter any of the enemy. Dugouts were bombed and the parties began to withdraw to our line again at 12.20 a.m. The barrage stopped at 12.40 a.m. There was very little retaliation by the enemy except on the fronts of the Battalions on our flanks. During the withdrawal the enemy opened rifle and machine gun fire from LOCUST Trenches. It appeared as if the enemy had evacuated his forward posts when our barrage opened, and retired to his main line of defence. Although the raid did not produce any prisoners the lessons learnt were most useful. The majority of the men had never before advanced under a	

Army Form C. 2118.

WAR DIARY
or
INTELLIGENCE SUMMARY.
(Erase heading not required.)

Instructions regarding War Diaries and Intelligence Summaries are contained in F. S. Regs., Part II. and the Staff Manual respectively. Title pages will be prepared in manuscript.

Place	Date	Hour	Summary of Events and Information	Remarks and references to Appendices
	8th	3.5 a.m.	barrage, and the ease with which they were able to follow it gave them confidence for future operations. All the arrangements, barrages, etc. worked exactly as planned, and the previous rehearsals at ACHEUX proved invaluable. Captain G.W. McGowran was in command and 2/Lieuts E. Kinrade and F.I. Constantine were in charge of two of the platoons. Our casualties were 3 killed and 5 wounded. No men were missing. Battn H.Q. during the raid were in BOVEN Trench, South of AUCHONVILLERS. After the raid, "D" Company returned to ACHEUX. Enemy opened a heavy bombardment on area of Brigade on our right. Otherwise normal activity.	
BEAUSSART	9th	9 p.m.	Battalion relieved by 15th Durham Light Infantry, and on relief occupied positions West of BEAUSSART in Brigade Reserve.	
MAILLY-MAILLET	10th	9 p.m.	Battn relieved 12/13th Northumberland Fusiliers in PURPLE SYSTEM of trenches North and North East of MAILLY MAILLET. "D" Company rejoined Battalion from ACHEUX. "B" Coy on right, "G" Coy in centre, "D" Coy on left, with "A" Coy in support. Battn H.Q. in Brewery in MAILLY MAILLET.	
	11th		Normal	
	12th		do } No change.	
	13th		do	
	14th		Enemy vacated his forward system opposite front of Brigade. 12/13th Northumberland Fusiliers advanced as far as WALKER and LUMINOUS Avenues, but little hostile opposition being encountered. Hostile artillery activity above normal against BEAUMONT HAMEL and vicinity. Battalion remained in MAILLY MAILLET.	

Army Form C. 2118.

WAR DIARY
or
INTELLIGENCE SUMMARY.
(Erase heading not required.)

Place	Date	Hour	Summary of Events and Information	Remarks and references to Appendices
	15th		Normal. Since the beginning of the month enemy shelled every night with gas shells battery positions West of MAILLY MAILLET.	
	16th	8.p.m.	Battalion moved forward to take over front system from 15th D.L.I. "A" Company took over right outpost company in vicinity of Q.12.b.7.5. "B" Company took over left outpost company in vicinity of Q.6.c.9.2. The situation of the two outpost companies on taking over was obscure. Orders were issued for "A" Company to establish a picquet line from LUMINOUS AVENUE, Q.12.b.70.45 to R.1.c.3.2 with three platoons, and with one platoon and Company H.Q. at Q.12.b.6.5, and for "B" Company to establish a picquet line from left of "A" Company to Q.6.d.9.9 with two platoons and with one platoon in support at Q.6.a.2.3, and one platoon and Company H.Q. at Q.6.c.9.2 in LOT TRENCH. This line was established by dawn. "B" and "C" Companies occupied LEVANT Support and LOCUST Support. "Don Q.10.b.9.7 - Q.11.c.8.2. "B" Company on left and "C" Company on right. This line was the line of resistance and "B" and "C" Companies proceeded orders to maintain this line. Battn.H.Q. at Western end of V" Ravine, Q.10.c.6.7. Relay Posts were established in Ravine at Q.12.c.2.5. The enemy were holding BEAUCOURT with screens posts in LUMINOUS AVENUE at R.1.a.1.4 and at R.1.a.6.2. His main line North of BEAUCOURT appeared to be along high ground in R.2 with posts along sunk road R.1.b.7 and d. Our patrols found enemy posts forward of this line in the vicinity of ARTILLERY LANE. The Brigade on our right had posts in the vicinity of Q.16.b.9.9 and 42nd Division on our left had posts in Q.6.b. Definite communication was not established on our flanks until the following night.	

Army Form C. 2118.

WAR DIARY
or
INTELLIGENCE SUMMARY.
(Erase heading not required.)

Instructions regarding War Diaries and Intelligence Summaries are contained in F. S. Regs., Part II. and the Staff Manual respectively. Title pages will be prepared in manuscript.

Place	Date	Hour	Summary of Events and Information	Remarks and references to Appendices
"Y" RAVINE Q.10.d.5.7.	17th		Enemy quiet all day. His machine guns were active during the night, especially from direction of BEAUCOURT AND THIEPVAL Ridge. All fire delivered on our front line was enfilade fire from right flank. Capt. H.W. Wirth and one sergeant went to visit outpost line and were bombed by enemy post. These two did not return and are missing.	
	18th 5 a.m.		The enemy opened a heavy bombardment on our outpost line. The heaviest fire, however, was concentrated on our left front about R.1.a. and d. A party of the enemy then attempted a raid on our left positions. As the mist cleared about 100 of the enemy were seen about R.1.d.1.7., and it is uncertain whether the enemy were merely attempting a raid or were intending to gain possession of the high ground held by our outposts. The enemy gained no footing in our line and retired quickly as soon as our line opened fire. "D" Company suffered several casualties owing to being exposed to heavy machine gun fire from their right flank. 2/Lieut F.L. Constantine was wounded. (since died of wounds.)	
			The enemy's artillery during the day was considerably more active, attention being specially paid to "Y" Ravine and STATION Road.	
	19th 9 p.m.		"B" and "C" Companies relieved "D" and "A" Companies respectively in the outpost line. On relief "D" Company took over position in LEVANT Support vacated by "B" Company. "A" Company with two platoons occupied position in LOCUST Support vacated by "C" Company and established a post strength one platoon in Ravine at Q.12.d.5.2. As Brigade on right had withdrawn their posts in vicinity of Q.16.b.9.9., the remaining platoon occupied Ravine, Q.12.c.2.5. in support. One company, 1st Bn Lincolnshire Regiment, attached to Battalion; 2 platoons occupied LEVANT Support on right of "D" Company; 2 platoons in BEAUMONT Trench, Q.10.d.5.9.	
			The enemy increased his artillery activity, especially between 9 p.m. and midnight, fire directed mainly on "Y" Ravine and STATION. Hostile machine guns very active throughout the night enfilading our	

Army Form C. 2118.

WAR DIARY
or
INTELLIGENCE SUMMARY.
(Erase heading not required.)

Instructions regarding War Diaries and Intelligence Summaries are contained in F. S. Regs., Part II. and the Staff Manual respectively. Title pages will be prepared in manuscript.

Place	Date	Hour	Summary of Events and Information	Remarks and references to Appendices
	20th	5 a.m.	lines from right flank. Battn H.Q. moved to BEAUMONT Reserve Trench, 500 yards S.E. of AUCHONVILLERS. Enemy quiet during the day except on parties moving up to front line along LUCK ALLEY, who were sniped from THIEPVAL Ridge.	

Army Form C. 2118.

WAR DIARY
or
INTELLIGENCE SUMMARY.

(Erase heading not required.)

Instructions regarding War Diaries and Intelligence Summaries are contained in F. S. Regs., Part II. and the Staff Manual respectively. Title pages will be prepared in manuscript.

Place	Date	Hour	Summary of Events and Information	Remarks and references to Appendices
			2nd Battn LINCOLNSHIRE REGIMENT	
			ACCOUNT OF OPERATIONS	
			From 6 p.m. August 29th, 1918, to midnight, August 29th/30th/18.	Reference Maps: Puis'eux 57dS.E. 1/10,000. 57dS.E. 1/20,000. 57dS.W. 1/20,000.
Nr AUCHONVILLERS	29th	6 p.m.	Battalion disposed as follows :-	Orders with B.M. at 5.45 p.m. on August 21st.
			Batln H.Q. BEAUMONT Reserve Trench, 500 yards S.E. of AUCHONVILLERS.	Bn H.Q. Lt Col. E.P. Lloyd, D.S.O.
			"A" Company. In Support. 2 platoons in LEVANT Trenches, 300 yards south of BEAUMONT HAMEL. 1 Platoon in Ravine, 600 yards south of BEAUMONT HAMEL on STATION Road. 1 platoon in Ravine near River ANCRE, Q.12.d.5.3.	Capt. Aug. M.C. J.E. Oliver M.C. Lt R.P. P-ce- Signalling Offr 2/Lt D. Savage L.G. Officer. 2/Lt W.E. Durrin Intelligence Offr
			"B" Company. Left Outpost. On high ground along BEAUCOURT - SERRE Road in Q.6.d. Had platoons at Blockouts with 2 platoons in support	"A" Company Capt P.M. Levin Commdg. 2/Lt J.M. Sweeney " G.B. Childs " C.A. Russell
			"C" Company. Right Outpost. On slope between BEAUCOURT - SERRE Road and BEAUCOURT Road in Q.12.b. 3 platoons in picquet line and 1 platoon in support.	
			"D" Company. In Support. In LEVANT Trenches.	
			The enemy held positions along the Battalion front about 300 yards away on right flank, which was covered by a Lewis and a Machine Gun Post in LUMINOUS AVENUE to cover BEAUCOURT. (Position of this Post was Q.12.b.9.4., about 150 yards from our right post.) Orders received for 62nd Infantry Brigade to take part at dawn on the following day in an attack on the enemy's positions in conjunction	

Army Form C. 2118.

WAR DIARY
or
INTELLIGENCE SUMMARY.
(Erase heading not required.)

Place	Date	Hour	Summary of Events and Information	Remarks and references to Appendices
			Sheet 2	
			With Brigades and Battalions on the flanks. The total frontage of the attack was to be about 9 miles. The success of the initial attack in the 51st Divisional Sector and the possibility of carrying further phases depended to a great extent on the capture of BAUCOURT. This village was on the right flank of the outpost line held by the Battalion, and its capture within half an hour of the attack was of the battle enabled the remaining Battalions in the Brigade (1st Lincolnshire Regiment and 12/13th Northumberland Fusiliers) to advance and reach their objectives.	B. Compon. Lt. J. Da.... Comdg.... 2/Lt. R. A. Ch.. 2/Lt. A. P.... Lt. W. Brown M.C. C. Compon. Capt. J.J. Billiat. Ca.. 2/Lt. R. Sharp.. " J.A. Groves " L.C. Lt. G.P. Walton.
		9 p.m.	Enemy attempted but unsuccessful raid on the left picquet of "B" Company. Enemy strength estimated at 50. The enemy attempted to push both flanks but was held by the steady fire of the post. A party out at the left flank under 2/Lieut A. T..... caused the enemy absence to	D. Compon. Capt. W.D. Perrins. 2/Lt. Griffin. 2/Lt. E.S...... " Rich.. bon.. 2/Lt. E.A. Gould. 2/Lt. M. Trot. C.F Rev.. M. Trot. D.S.O. & C. Capt. N.P.O. Scott, R.A.M.C.
	21st	12.15 a.m.	Enemy opened an intensive bombardment of the area occupied by the 2 support companies, "A" and "D" Companies, and the communications leading to the front line. This lasted until 2.15 a.m. and considerably interfered with these 2 companies, while they were preparing to move forward. Several minor casualties were sustained, but the remainder of the men, although all were suffering from the effects of the gas shelling, carried on at duty. Battalion Headquarters and "A" and "D" Companies moved forward to positions of assembly ready for the assault. Battn H.Q. moved to LUMINOUS AVENUE, Q.12.b.4.7. "A" Company formed up on in Sunkin North East from LUMINOUS AVENUE with their right at Q.12.b.8.6. "D" Company formed up on a line running South West from LUMINOUS AVENUE in prolongation of "A" Company. Both companies were on a frontage of 100 yards with 2 platoons in leading wave and 2 platoons in second wave, 25 yards between platoons. Each platoon had 2 sections in front with L.G. Section on flank immediately behind. A bombing party of "C" Coy	
LUMINOUS AVENUE.	"	2 a.m.		

Army Form C. 2118.

WAR DIARY
or
INTELLIGENCE SUMMARY.
(Erase heading not required.)

Instructions regarding War Diaries and Intelligence Summaries are contained in F. S. Regs., Part II. and the Staff Manual respectively. Title pages will be prepared in manuscript.

Place	Date	Hour	Summary of Events and Information	Remarks and references to Appendices
			Sheet 3	
			formed up in LUMINOUS AVENUE between "A" and "D" Companies.	
			The morning was ideal for the forming up, as a thick mist hid all movement, and the smoke barrage arranged was consequently cancelled. The enemy post at Q.12.b.9.4. apparently heard the men forming up and opened fire, but orders were given for a Trench Mortar's fire a few yards at the post and no further hindrance was caused.	
		5.35 a.m.	The companies completed their forming up by 5.35 a.m.	
		5.45 "	Zero hour for the attack on BEAUCOURT was 5.45 a.m., at which hour 12 Stokes Guns opened a barrage on enemy post at Q.12.b.9.4. and selected targets behind. This fire was well directed and kept the enemy from firing back as well as driving him into his deep dugouts. The Stokes Mortar barrage lifted as the troops advanced, finally stopping at 5.53 a.m. At 5.45 a.m. a Hurricane bombardment of light calibre guns was put down for 8 minutes on to BEAUCOURT ruins.	
			At zero hour exactly, "A" and "D" Companies, under cover of this bombardment, moved forward to the assault. The bombing party of "C" Company under 2/Lieut R. Sharpe rushed the enemy post at Q.12.b.9.4., capturing 8 prisoners and a machine gun. This allowed "A" and "D" Companies to move forward without a check. So eager were the men that they were able to keep close up to the last moving barrage. "A" Company advanced, keeping LUMINOUS AVENUE on their right, and met little opposition until reaching RAILWAY Road where a machine gun on the last plank end the enemy retired. "A" Company then moved forward to the other plank end the enemy retired. "A" Company then moved forward to the railway which was then consolidated.	
			"D" Company advanced, keeping LUMINOUS AVENUE on their left. The leading wave pushed ahead and reached RAILWAY Road with but little opposition; the 2 platoons following encountered the enemy coming out of the numerous deep dugouts. These were bombed and many taken prisoners. A party of the enemy were seen on the right flank in RAILWAY	

WAR DIARY
or
INTELLIGENCE SUMMARY.
(Erase heading not required.)

Army Form C. 2118.

Place	Date	Hour	Summary of Events and Information	Remarks and references to Appendices
			Sheet 4.	
			Road, and these, after being fired on by Lewis Guns, disappeared. The Left Lewis platoon of "D" Company lost direction owing to RAILWAY Halt and proceeded too far East.—heads in BEAUCOURT at Q.7.d.7.8. This platoon, as it turned out, was most useful in guarding the left flank.	
	10 a.m.		There was a short delay in the ruins of BEAUCOURT while dugouts and small parties of the enemy were cleared up, and the 2 platoons then captured were to be utilized. This order "D" Company to consolidate the line of Q.1.b.1/4.7 and "D" Company to form a support line along RAILWAY Road, being in close touch with the left flank. The total number of prisoners captured by the 2 companies was 3 officers and 90 other ranks, who belonged to the 68th R.I. Regiment, 16 R. Division.	
			By this time the 1st Lincolns considerable trouble was caused from Machine gun fire from LOUPART SUPPORT, South of River ANCRE, and throughout the afternoon this position was heavily shelled.	
			At 3.30 p.m. 12/13th Northumberland Fusiliers pushed patrols across to the South side of the River ANCRE, but made but little progress owing to machine gun fire from THIEPVAL Ridge.	
			At 8.45 p.m. "D" Company were able to get in touch with 1st East Yorks at R.6.a.45.95.	
	2 p.m.		At 3 a.m. on August 22nd "A" and "D" Companies were relieved by 1 Company Northumberland Fusiliers (12/13th), and marched to ACHEUX. It was necessary owing to the large number of men who had been gassed. The 2 companies holding the outpost line, "B" and "C" Companies, were ordered to assemble and move forward to the line reached by the 1st Lincolnshire Regiment in their advance. "C" Company moved forward on the right and "B" Company on the left. Both companies moving in artillery formation. On reaching the valley in R.1.b. and d., the 2 companies passed through the 1st Lincolnshire Regiment and advanced to	

Army Form C. 2118.

WAR DIARY
or
INTELLIGENCE SUMMARY.
(Erase heading not required.)

Instructions regarding War Diaries and Intelligence Summaries are contained in F.S. Regs., Part II. and the Staff Manual respectively. Title pages will be prepared in manuscript.

Place	Date	Hour	Summary of Events and Information	Remarks and references to Appendices
			Sheet 5	
		7.30 p.m.	the sunk road in R.3.c.	
		8 p.m.	Position in sunk road consolidated. The position was enfiladed by direct machine gun, rifle and trench mortar fire from GRANDCOURT, and owing to 42nd Division on our left not being up in line considerable trouble was caused by parties of the enemy working round and on the left flank of "B" Company. Lieut G.P. Walton killed.	
Ravine, R.1.d.6.8.	22nd	1 a.m.	One platoon, D Company, 12/13th Northumberland Fusiliers, came up on the left flank of "B" Company. Battalion H.Q. moved to R.1.d.6.8. and at 5 a.m. Front line was under command of Lieut Col. E.P. Lloyd, D.S.O. Troops in front line - 1 company 1st Lincolnshire Regt on right from R.3.c.5.1. - R.3.c.5.3. "C" and "B" Companies, 2nd Lincolnshire Regt R.3.c.5.3. - R.3.c.4.5. in centre, and a platoon of "D" Company, 12/13th Northumberland Fusiliers, on left. Remainder of "D" Company, 12/13th Northumberland Fusiliers, at R.2.d.5.8. 1st Lincolnshire Regt. held a	
		5 a.m.	line about 400 yards in rear. Enemy attacked platoon of "D" Coy. 12/13th Northumble Fus. on left flank and they were compelled to withdraw. No.8 platoon, "B" Company, was sent to form a defensive flank on the left, and was able to form a defensive flank there, and thus prevented the enemy from completely working round the left flank. At the same time the enemy worked up the ANCRE Valley on the right flank in small parties, but were dispersed by Lewis Gun fire.	
		1.30 p.m.	Remaining 3 platoons, "D" Coy, 12/13th Northumberland Fusiliers, together with a detachment of North Irish Horse under Lieut E.A. Atkinson with 3 Lewis Guns were sent forward to clear up situation and protect left flank of "B" Company. These gained touch with 42nd Division and considerably eased the situation there.	
		7.30 p.m.	Under a light barrage of Trench Mortars the enemy attacked our front	

WAR DIARY
or
INTELLIGENCE SUMMARY

Army Form C. 2118.

Place	Date	Hour	Summary of Events and Information	Remarks and references to Appendices
			Sheet 6.	
		11 p.m.	He came up the ANCRE Valley and then extended Northwards when 300 yards away. A few at within 30 yards of our position in the sunk road and these not killed dispersed. Over fifty dead were counted next day on the front. During the attack troops on the right flank were driven in, but the right platoon of "C" Company were able to restore the situation. The attack also developed on the front of "B" Company, but the steady fire of our men completely repulsed the enemy. "B" Company 12/13th Northumberland Fusiliers, and detachment of North Irish Horse Withdrawn.	
	24th.10.16		42nd Division on our left advanced across our front into BEAUMONT	
		2 p.m.	1st Lincolnshire Batt. at 12/13th Northumberland Fusiliers less "C" Coy. River NCRE to BOOM Valley. East of GRANDCOURT	
BOOM VALLEY R.11.c.1.4.		7 p.m.	"B" and "C" Companies, Batt. H.Q. and ANCRE as position in BOOM Valley, R.11.c.1.4. "B" and "C" Companies moved and took up a position Lon. Bart MIRAUMONT Road from R.18.a.3.6. - R.18.a.3.9. with Battn H.Q. and detachment North Irish Horse at R.17.b.5.5. 1st Lincolnshire Battn less "B" Battalion and 12/13th Northumberland Fusiliers on left less "C" Company BEAUMONT Road.	2/Lt A. Gasman 2/Lt V.W. Mansonring and 2/Lt E. Thoup joined.
	25.9.16 a.m.		1st Lincolnshire Batt. on right and 12/13th Northumberland Fusiliers on left moved forward to LA SARS. "B" and "C" Companies with Battn H.Q. and detachment N.I.H. 11th Horse moved East of the Railway direction LE SARS. Operation. On moving up enemy shelled direction as difficult to maintain but the 1st East Lance kept in touch. A feature of the advance was the FAST pace at which the Battalion moved. On reaching ANCRE at R.14.a.5.5., the 2 Leading Battalions were held	

Army Form C. 2118.

WAR DIARY
or
INTELLIGENCE SUMMARY.
(Erase heading not required.)

Place	Date	Hour	Summary of Events and Information	Remarks and references to Appendices
1000 yds W. of Le SARS.		8.30 p.m.	Sheet 7. up by heavy machine gun fire from the ridge in M.15.c. A patrol was sent out from "C" Company, to gain touch with 7th Lincolnshire Regt (17th Division) on our left, in COURCELETTE. "B" Company moved up the West along valley to M.15.a.9.8. and then due East in order to pull in and get astride M.15.c. This movement was partially successful, the enemy on the ridge of the hill being at once reinforced and the machine gun in M.15.c. when compelled to withdraw. One machine gun was captured here. The remainder of the Brigade were then able to continue the advance.	
		10 a.m.	"B" Company advanced with 12/13th Northumberland Fusiliers on right and pushed Northern outskirts of L SARS without further opposition.	
		11 a.m.	The advance was then continued to BLUE CUT, M.18.b.5.7. "B" Company then moved North down BLUE CUT into Le BARQUE and took away counter-attack.	
		1 p.m.	Throughout the day "B" Company was continually engaged with the enemy in Le BARQUE, but were able to maintain their position about N.7.a.1.2.	
East of Le SARS.		2 p.m.	"B" Company and Batn H.Q., M.16.d.5.7., had to take up a position running North and South through the PIPPE in consequence of enemy parties being seen coming over high ground in M.24 between right of Brigade and 17th Division on right. 64th Infantry Bde also moved forward to fill this gap and the position was restored.	
		5 p.m.	Batn H.Q. detachment North Irish Horse and "C" Company moved to valley about M.22.b.4.8. in support to 6th Leicesters who were holding a line through SITE OF MILL, Valley heavily shelled all day.	
		10 p.m.	"B" Company was relieved by A Company, Artists Rifles, and re-organised in trench in M.16.d. just South of L BARQUE. Batn H.Q., detachment North Irish Horse and "C" Company moved to	Joined 2/Lt. W. Joyce, " " R.H. Brown
N. of Le SARS.	20th	7 p.m.		

Army Form C. 2118.

WAR DIARY
or
INTELLIGENCE SUMMARY.
(Erase heading not required.)

Instructions regarding War Diaries and Intelligence Summaries are contained in F. S. Regs., Part II. and the Staff Manual respectively. Title pages will be prepared in manuscript.

Place	Date	Hour	Summary of Events and Information	Remarks and references to Appendices
BUTTE de WARLENCOURT.	27th	8 p.m.	Chap. 8. trenches North of L. SARS. where "A" and "B" Companies relieved Battalion. Battalion in Brigade Reserve. Lieut H.P.T. Pryce wounded.	
WARLENCOURT.	28th	10 p.m.	Battalion moved to trenches East of BUTTE de WARLENCOURT in Brigade Reserve. Battalion relieved by 7th Leicesters and went into trenches South of WARLENCOURT. West Brigade in Divisional Reserve.	2/Lt C.H.S. Rand joined.
WARLENCOURT.	29th		Battalion remained at WARLENCOURT in Divisional Reserve. Casualties during operations 6 p.m. August 20th to midnight August 29th/30th. OFFICERS. OTHER RANKS. Killed. Lieut G.R. Walton. Killed. 21. Died of Wounds. 2/Lieut F.T. Constantine. Wounded. 74. Wounded. Lieut H.P.T. Pryce. Missing. 15. Missing. Nil. This does not include casualties from shelling on night August 20th/21st. 3 officers. 90 other ranks. Captures during operations 6 p.m. August 20th to midnight August 29th/30th. 4 machine guns.	

Army Form C. 2118.

WAR DIARY
or
INTELLIGENCE SUMMARY.
(Erase heading not required.)

Instructions regarding War Diaries and Intelligence Summaries are contained in F.S. Regs., Part II. and the Staff Manual respectively. Title pages will be prepared in manuscript.

Place	Date	Hour	Summary of Events and Information	Remarks and references to Appendices
HARLEMCOURT	30th 31st		Battalion remained in Divisional Reserve.) do.	Reinforcements amount to 200 other ranks received. The two days spent in re-organising and resting.

The Battalion has not been out of the line since July 24th, and from August 17th to August 27th has been in the front line and actively engaged with the enemy.

Despite the hardships and fatigue of this period, the men have behaved in a manner beyond praise and have responded to all calls in a cheerful and willing manner.

Owing to the Battalion having recently suffered heavy casualties, drafts received during the past six weeks have totalled about 650 (about 60% of fighting strength), giving but little time for organisation or training, but all ranks have shown fine spirit and determination, which has on every occasion ensured success.

The weather has been exceptionally fine, but little rain having been experienced, and the health of the men has been good. A large proportion of men reporting sick has been due to men slightly gassed feeling the effects some days after.

The operations from August 17th have greatly raised the moral of the men, who are now prepared for any exceptional strain which they may be called upon to undergo. Every man is satisfied that it requires several Boches to equal one of ours. The successful assault of BEAUCOURT has given the men confidence to tackle any further difficult operation.

The Battalion is now equipped with 30 Lewis Guns - 2 with each platoon and 4 at Battn H.Q.

The 21st Division, to which the Battalion belongs, is in the V Corps, commanded by Lieut-General G.D. Shute, CB, CMG, and in the Third Army, commanded by General Hon. Sir J.H.G. Byng, K.C.B., K.C.M.G., M.V.O.

Army Form C. 2118.

WAR DIARY
or
INTELLIGENCE SUMMARY.
(Erase heading not required.)

Instructions regarding War Diaries and Intelligence Summaries are contained in F. S. Regs., Part II. and the Staff Manual respectively. Title pages will be prepared in manuscript.

Place	Date	Hour	Summary of Events and Information	Remarks and references to Appendices
			TOTAL CASUALTIES DURING THE MONTH OF AUGUST, 1916.	
			Officers. Other Ranks.	
			Killed - (Lieut G.F. Walton) 1 32	This does not
			Wounded - {2/Lt F.I. Constantine} 2 125	include men
			{Lieut H.E.W. Fryce}	gassed.
			Missing - A/Capt. R.W. Firth. 1 5	
			2/Lieut F.I. Constantine since died of wounds.	
			Emerged Lieut. Colonel Comdg. 2 Lincolnshire Regt.	

Army Form W.3091.

Cover for Documents.

Nature of Enclosures.

War Diary
of
2nd Bn Lincolnshire Regiment
for period
1st September 1918 to 30th September 1918.

Notes, or Letters written.

Army Form C. 2118.

WAR DIARY
or
INTELLIGENCE SUMMARY.
(Erase heading not required.)

Place	Date	Hour	Summary of Events and Information	Remarks and references to Appendices
			War Diary for period 1st September 1916 to 30th September 1916.	Ref. D/c.S.W. 1/20,000. 57cS.E. 1/20,000.
WARLENCOURT	1st		Battn H.Q. at WARLENCOURT, a.10.D.45.15. "B" and "D" Companies in Sunken Road south of WARLENCOURT. "A" and "D" Companies in trenches North East of LE SARS, M.6.6.4. in Divisional Reserve.	
		11 a.m.	Battalion Church Parade.	
N.E. of Le SARS	2nd	2.30 p.m.	Moved forward to SUNKEN ROAD, South of LE BARQUE, with Battn. H.Q. at M.17.b. "B" Company in support in trench, M.17.D. "A" Company on left, "D" Company in Centre, "C" Company on right, along Sunken Road in M.10 & M.24. These three companies held line each with 4 platoon posts.	
		7.20 p.m.	Battn ordered to move forward to GUEUDECOURT in Corps Reserve, and counter-attack Battalion. Positions taken up as follows at 9.30 p.m. "A" Company - N.27.4.6.5 "B" Company - N.28.c.4.1. "C" Company - N.34.a.6.6. } Along Sunken Road with Battn H.Q. "D" Company - N.34.c.6.9. } at N.34.a.35.55. Day exceptionally quiet.	
S.E. of GUEUDECOURT	3rd	6 p.m.	Battalion still in Corps Reserve. Detachment of North Irish Horse under about Stevens returned to unit.	
do	4th	6 a.m.	Brigade ordered to move to O.20.a.2.9, 300 yards South of LESBOEUFS, 12/13th Northumberland Fusiliers on left, 2nd Lincolns in Centre, 1st Lincolns on right. Route - Through THANNOY - ROSSIGNOL "A" Coy left - O.21.a. "D" Coy right - O.21.c.	

Army Form C. 2118.

WAR DIARY
or
INTELLIGENCE SUMMARY.
(Erase heading not required.)

Place	Date	Hour	Summary of Events and Information	Remarks and references to Appendices
N.W. of ROCQUIGNY.	5th	7.20 p.m.	Battn H.Q. - U.21.a. North West of ROCQUIGNY. Companies were in the open and were prepared to occupy trench line running between BRIASTRE and ROCQUIGNY.	Officers present with Bn at 7.20pm Lt Col E.r. Lloyd, D.S.O., Commdg. Capt. J.P. Clinge, Adjt. M.O. 2/Lt W.A. Deavin. Intellige Officer. 2/Lt H.V. Joyce. Signalling Officer. 2/Lt T.D. Stewart, L.G. Officer.
	6th	4.30 a.m.	S.E. of MANANCOURT. 62nd Brigade ordered to relieve 116th Brigade in front line Route - ROCQUIGNY - LE MESNIL - MANANCOURT. 2nd Lincolns in front line relieved 17th Royal Welsh Fusiliers. 1st Lincolns on left along CANAL DU NORD, V.19. One section, M.G.C. attached to 2nd Lincolns, under 2/Lieut SHARMAN. (four guns). Dispositions of Companies :- Battn H.Q. - D.19.b.6.8. "A". "D". "B". "C". Road - V.14.c.2.9. to V.19.b.9.0.	"A" Coy. 2/Lt R.M. Irvine. Commdg.
S.E. of MANANCOURT.		10 a.m.	1 platoon of "D" Company sent forward to prolong line to N.W. of 9th Essex Regt. V.22.a.3.0. - V.16.a.4.0. Another platoon of "D" Company moved forward and these two platoons occupied trench from B.22.b.6.0. - V.16.d.8.2.	2/Lt G.W. Stockwin. 2/Lt G. Tayler. 2/Lt A. Cox. "B" Coy.
		11 a.m.	9th Essex went forward and occupied trench in V.22.d. All four platoons of "D" Coy occupied trench from V.22.b.6.0. to V.16.d.c.c. Moving forward with 9th Essex on right. "A" Company occupied FAUCON trench, V.22.a.3.0. to V.16.a.4.4. "B" Company occupied Sunken road, V.21.b.5.0. to V.15.d.6.4.	Capt. J. Dawson, M.C. Commdg.
		2 p.m.	Battn H.Q. moved to Sunken road, V.15.d.6.0. "D" Company pushed forward patrols to line of road V.23.b.1.0. to V.18.c.1.9.	2/Lt E. Troup. 2/Lt F. Archer, L.A. Lt J.W. Brown.
		2.30 p.m. 3 p.m.	Remainder of "D" Coy moved to line of road as above. "A" Coy moved to trench vacated by "D" Company, V.22.b.6.0. to V.16.d.6.5.	

WAR DIARY
or
INTELLIGENCE SUMMARY.
(Erase heading not required.)

Army Form C. 2118.

Place	Date	Hour	Summary of Events and Information	Remarks and references to Appendices
N.W. of ELSOM COPSE	6th	3.15 p.m.	"C" Company moved to FAUCON trench, vacated by "A" Company.	"C" Coy.
			"D" Coy sent patrols to gain line East of SOREL le GRAND, W.19.Central. Touch maintained with Battn on right (of 12th Divsn) but 1st Lincolns were not yet up, in leftight opposition. Snipers and M.G. fire from FINS, also from right front.	2/Lt R. Sharpe. 2/Lt A. Carman. 2/Lt V. Manwaring. 2/Lt J.A. Graves, M.G.
			Near M.Q. at V.19.b.5.7. moved from C.18 (57c S.W.)	
		4 p.m.	"D" Coy moved forward to spur running E. of SOREL le GRAND, W.13.c.5.5. - W.19.c.1.5. which they held as outpost line for the night.	"D" Coy. Capt. C.W.McCennan. Commdg.
			"A" Coy moved up to road vacated by "D" Coy and found defensive flank facing N.E. in V.15.c.	
			"C" Coy moved to trench vacated by "A" Coy.	2/Lt C.H.S. Rand.
			"B" Coy moved to trench V.22.b.5.0. to V.16.d.3.4.	2/Lt F.H. Breen.
			Battn H.Q. moved to trench V.23.a.0.8.	2/Lt R.H. Taylor.
			1st Lincolns moved to high ground North of FINS V.6.b. and d. Touch gained with 1st Lincolns on left in FINS.	Cpt W.P.G. Scott, R.A.M.C.
		7 p.m.	Companies moved forward into position ready for continuing advance at daybreak.	Cpt (Rev) M. Tren, D.S.O., L.C. (C.F.)
V.23.a.0.6.	7th	4.30 a.m.	"B" Coy. detailed to lead advance, moved up to line with "D" Coy.	
			"C" Coy to Sunken Road V.24.d.5.0. "A" Coy to Sunken Rd V.23.b.8.0	
			Battn H.Q., 1 section of M.G's and detachment of Light T.M.B. moved to QUARRY, J.24.a.6.6. (Lt S.G. Taylor.)	
		6.20 a.m.	Move complete and Battn ready to move forward.	
		7.20 a.m.	Battn moved forward and leading Company ("B" Coy) after advancing 800 yards on to ridge, W.20.c. Were met with heavy machine gun fire from South end of NEUDICOURT and high ground South of village. Our advance here was stopped until 12th Division had made good high ground W.26.c.	
			Two leading platoons of "B" Coy pushed forward patrols and the	

WAR DIARY
or
INTELLIGENCE SUMMARY.
(Erase heading not required.)

Army Form C. 2118.

Place	Date	Hour	Summary of Events and Information	Remarks and references to Appendices
	7th		4.	
			remaining two platoons moved forward, one moving round wide on each flank. "C" Coy moved up into close support to "B" Coy. The deployment from Artillery formation by "B" and "C" Companies was carried out in perfect manner.	
		5.50 a.m.	Our artillery shelled line held by enemy machine guns.	
		9.30 a.m.	Our artillery ceased and "B" Company advanced to high ground, W.2.a., the enemy withdrawing. The enemy suffered many casualties here.	
			"C" Coy followed on to high ground behind "B" Coy.	
			"A" Coy remained on high ground W.20.c.	
			"D" Coy retired original position.	
			"B" Coy reached objective trench W.22.c.	
			"C" Coy closed up to road W.21.d.1.2.	
			"A" Company occupied road South of HEUDICOURT from Brickyard W.26.b.7.0.	
		12 noon.	"D" Company moved to valleys W.20.d.	
			Battn H.Q. moved to Brickyard.	
			Considerable shelling of whole area occupied by Battn, large proportion of sneezing gas shells.	
			Touch maintained with 6th R.W. Kents on right (12th Div.) but position of 1st Lincolns on left not clear.	
			2/Lt R. Sharpe and 2/Lt J.A. Graves, M.C. wounded.	
			"A" Company moved and took over line held by "B" Company preparatory to further advances.	
			"B" Company moved into support in trenches immediately behind "A" Company.	
		3 p.m.	"D" Coy moved to position vacated by "A" Company.	
			During advance 4 officers (Lieut J.W. Brown, M.C. and Rev (Capt.) M. Tree, D.S.O., M.C.) wounded. Approximately 90 O.R. casualties.	
			About 65 % of casualties due to M.G. fire, remainder being shell fire	

WAR DIARY
or
INTELLIGENCE SUMMARY.
(Erase heading not required.)

Army Form C. 2118.

Place	Date	Hour	Summary of Events and Information	Remarks and references to Appendices
S. of NEUVCOURT	7th		Weather was very sultry, and rough going was very trying to the men.	
		7 p.m.	Intermittent heavy hostile shelling throughout afternoon. "C" Company ordered to form defensive flank with one platoon at road junction, W.22.c.1.6., facing North, to protect left flank as 1st Lincolns had not been able to make good RÉVÉLON RIDGE. 4 machine guns also placed in position near Bn H.Q. to cover RAILTON VALLEY.	
do	8th 5 a.m.		"A" and "B" Companies, 12/13th Northumberland Fusiliers, moved forward and assembled in trench occupied by "A" and "B" Companies, 2nd Lincolns, coming under orders of O.C., 2nd Lincolns, ready to advance in conjunction with attack by 58th Division on FEUZIÈRES, and protect left flank of 58th Division.	("A" Coy ordered to be ready to support 2 companies, 12/13 N.F. in order to maintain spur W.25.c. at all costs.
		7.30 a.m.	Artillery barrage opened and two companies, 12/13th Northumberland Fusiliers, advanced, both reaching their objectives "A" Coy, 12/13th N.F's - trenches S. of railway W.24.c. "B" " " " " N. " " W.23.b. During advance considerable machine gun fire from North and vicinity of CHAPEL HILL and from right front from North end of FEUZIÈRES. Hostile retaliation was not heavy. On reaching objectives, "A" and "B" Companies, 12/13th N.F's, consolidated, and "A" Company sent forward patrols along railway to W.24.d.	"A" Coy (badly) Lieut Sherwood. (wounded 8.9.18) "B" Coy (badly) Cpt Rutherford. (wounded 8.9.18)
		11 a.m.	"A" Company, 12/13th N.F. reported they could not gain touch with 58th Division on right, and were compelled to withdraw from railway in W.24.d., owing to the enemy working round both flanks, and direct M.G. fire from W.27.d.9.2.	
		2.30 p.m.	"A" Coy, 12/13th N.F. withdrew to trench W.23.Central, on right of "B" Coy, 12/13th N.F. owing to not being able to gain touch with 58th Division in trench W.23.d.	

WAR DIARY
or
INTELLIGENCE SUMMARY.
(Erase heading not required.)

Army Form C. 2118.

Place	Date	Hour	Summary of Events and Information	Remarks and references to Appendices
S. of HEBUTERNE	6th		2 Lewis Gun teams sent up to reinforce "A" Coy, 12/13th N.F. "C" Coy heavily gas-shelled and ordered in consequence to move to higher ground on right of "B" Coy in W.24.d.	2/Lt K.M. Irvine. to Hospital, gassed.
		5 p.m.	Our troops seen in vicinity of GENIN WELL COPSE No. 1, W.17.a. T.M. sent forward to "A" Company, 2nd Lincolns, to assist in protection of left flank. 2 Lewis Gun teams sent forward to "A" Coy, 12/13th N.F.	
	8th	1 a.m.	"A" Company relieved by "G" Coy, 12/13th N.F. relieved.	
		2 a.m.	"B" & "C" Companies relieved by "D" Coy, 12/13th N.F.	
		3 a.m.	Our artillery opened an intensive barrage on high ground North of our position, in conjunction with attack by 64th Infantry	
		4 a.m.	Brigade on CHAPEL HILL. This led to considerable hostile retaliation in our area, which considerably interfered with the movements of our companies on their way out. Command of sector passed to O.C., 12/13th N.F. On relief, Battn proceeded to billets in MANANCOURT, "D" Company marching off with "A" Company	
		5 a.m.	Since August 21st, 21st Division have driven enemy back a total distance of about 31 kilometres, from BEAUMONT HAMEL to PUZIEURES. During this period Battn has taken part in hard fighting during the first 10 days and last 3 days. from the night 5th/6th, Battn was fighting over and regaining the identical ground, over which it withdrew during the enemy's offensive in March, 1918, including the villages SOREL le GRAND and HEUDICOURT. Fighting on afternoon of Sept. 5th actually took place in same trenches which were held with great gallantry on March 22nd 1918. On being relieved, position held by Battn was only a few hundred yards short of the front line held on March 21st. The	

WAR DIARY
or
INTELLIGENCE SUMMARY.
(Erase heading not required.)

Army Form C. 2118.

Place	Date	Hour	Summary of Events and Information	Remarks and references to Appendices
			7.	
			knowledge that the battn was fighting over ground which had been given up in face of superior numbers and after hard fighting in march was the means of being a great incentive to the men, whose dash and eagerness regained in the face of considerable opposition a depth of 8000 yards in 24 hours	
MANANCOURT	10th		Remainder of the day was spent in rest, the men having been through most exhausting periods, but despite that fact and a long march to billets, the men arrived back very cheerful and quite ready to go forward again and continue the advance.	
			Remainder of Brigade came back to MANANCOURT and vicinity, whole brigade being in Divisional Reserve.	
			Prisoners captured by this battn since the beginning of September include men from the following Regiments.	
				Numbers.
			6th Cavalry Regt, 7th Division.	2
			2nd)	1
			403rd Regiment.)	
			377th Regiment.) 201st Division.	2
			21st Regiment.)	1
			14th Regiment.	2
			In addition, two parties of about 25 each were captured in HEUDICOURT. Prisoners appeared to be in a very poor state and their morale was low. In one case a party of 6 men belonging to 201st Division, 377th R.I.R., were sent to SACQUEMIE COPSE without an officer or a N.C.O. in charge and without any definite orders. They knew nothing as to the movements of their own Regiment or Division.	

WAR DIARY
or
INTELLIGENCE SUMMARY.
(Erase heading not required.)

Army Form C. 2118.

Place	Date	Hour	Summary of Events and Information	Remarks and references to Appendices
HEBUTERNE	11th		Battn still in Divisional Reserve.	
do	12th		do.	
do	13th		do.	
do	14th		do.	
do	15th	6 p.m.	Companies "A", "C" and "B" practised attack.	
do	16th	10 a.m. / 7 p.m.	Battn still in Divisional Reserve. Battn moved up to front line, relieving 1st Queen's (R.W.S.) Regt., 3rd Division. "B" Company relieved 1st Company, R.W.S. in KILN.—. – (front line) from W.28.d. K.24.c.5.9. (inclusive) to W.22.d.65.00. "A" "B" and "D" Companies moved to known pos., W.22.c. "A" Company to position held previously, at W.22.c. "C" Company by "B" Company, W.28.c. "D" Company in trench W.28.a. Companies moved in following order:- "B" "A" "C" "D" Rous – BLANCOURT – MURLU – QUARRY – HEBUTERNE to front line. Battn H.Q. – Brickyard –. of HEBUTERNE, K.31.c.1.1. Relief was complete at 12.15 a.m. 12/13th Northumberland Fus. took over trenches on our left and 2/2nd Londons were in occupation of trenches on our right.	ref. 5/6.6.2. 1/20,000.
do	17th		Day quiet on us, up to were being shelled and houses. HEBUTERNE and area to front of it. Very quiet during day, except for shelling of battery areas. The day was spent in making final arrangements for the attack on following morning. Battn H.Q. moved forward to Battle H.Q. in KILMAN AVENUE, W.28.b.5.5.	
S. of HEBUTERNE	18th	10 p.m. / 2 a.m.	Enemy opened heavy barrage on front line and high ground 1000 yards in rear, which lasted for 45 minutes. No infantry action followed. "B" Company, B area was heavily bombed by hostile aeroplanes. During remainder	

WAR DIARY
or
INTELLIGENCE SUMMARY.
(Erase heading not required.)

Army Form C. 2118.

Instructions regarding War Diaries and Intelligence Summaries are contained in F. S. Regs., Part II. and the Staff Manual respectively. Title pages will be prepared in manuscript.

Place	Date	Hour	Summary of Events and Information	Remarks and references to Appendices
N.22.b.5.0.		2 a.m.	of night there was intense gas shelling of area of Division on our right. "A", "C" and "D" Companies moved forward to Assembly Positions astride the RAILWAY at N.24.c.3.9. "C" Company on right in two lines with 2 platoons in each line, 1 platoon of each line on either side of RAILWAY. "D" Company in centre on left of "C" Company, and in similar formation. "B" Company was relieved by Batt. H.Q. Lewis Gun platoon and formed up on a 4 platoon frontage S. of RAILWAY, behind platoons of "C" Company. The formations of the platoons of all companies were 2 sections in front wave and L.G. section in second wave. 25 yards distance and interval between platoons of "B" Company. Total frontage of Battalion was 300 yards. Companies formed up on a previously laid tape line running N. and S. 50 yards in rear of front line. 12/15th R.F. formed up in similar formation on immediate left of Bas'n with 1st.Lincoln Regiment immediately on their left. The 2/2nd London (58th Division) formed up on our right S. of RAILWAY - RAILWAY Road, the Gap between the two Battalions being held by Batt. H.Q. Lewis Gun platoon. The advance to Assembly Positions was carried out under very adverse weather conditions. Heavy rain falling and very dark. All companies formed up ready for the assault.	Appendix A " B Officers at at 2.20 a.m. Battn H.Q. Lt.Col. E.F. Lloyd, DSO. Cmdg. Cpt J.R. Clingo. Adjutant. M.G. Lt. F.B. Stewart. Lewis Gun Offr. 2/Lt W.E. Deavin. Intelligce Offr. 2/Lt H.V. Joyce Sig. Officer
		3.5 a.m. 3.20 a.m.	2.30 hour for the attack was 3.20 a.m., at which hour it was still dark. The objective of the Brigade was Trench line running East of high Ground between TUDIES and VAUCELLETTE FARM. 1st objective of Batt. - VAUCE... SUPPORT. "A" Coy from N.19.c.3.5. to N.19.c.2.5. "B" Coy from right of "A" Coy along RAILWAY to N.19.c.4.0. "D" Coy from right of "B" Coy along RAILWAY just South of right of "B" Coy. "C" Coy - Junction of Road and RAILWAY just South of right of our 2nd and RAILWAY at N.24.d. 7.0. This was 1.0 projection of night plan. At ZERO hour a creeping barrage came down 200 yards in front of our	

WAR DIARY or INTELLIGENCE SUMMARY

Army Form C. 2118.

(Erase heading not required.)

Instructions regarding War Diaries and Intelligence Summaries are contained in F. S. Regs., Part II. and the Staff Manual respectively. Title pages will be prepared in manuscript.

Place	Date	Hour	Summary of Events and Information	Remarks and references to Appendices
		6.4..	Leading companies and moved forward at rate of 100 yards in four minutes. "A" and "B" Companies moved forward close behind this Barrage. "C" Company moving close behind "A" Company. Considerable M.G. opposition was encountered along Railway in W.27.d., but these M.G. posts were successfully dealt with and did not materially check the advance. There was very little rifle or rifle grenade reply. The 1st objective was found to be strongly held, but our men. The little resistance was and determined, overwhelmed and captured and killed the Germans. Several machine guns were taken here. These MG's at W.30.c.4.9 and W.12/21 M.F. on left also were dealt with. Garrisons of Trenches at N.28 and W.24.d.8.4. and at junction of Railway, strong in-particular of Loop Railway K.24.d.8.4 and at junction of Railway and Sunk Road at X.19.c.2.0. Barrage remained stationary for 10 minutes (Zero plus 42 to Zero plus 50) on line X.19.c.6.6. to X.19.c.5.0. On reaching 1st objective, 2nd wave of "A", "C" and "D" Companies moved forward to 2nd objective. "A" Company - 2 platoons. "B" Company - 2 platoons. to right of its objective. "C" Company - 2 platoons remained on 1st objective. Remaining 2 platoons moved to junction of Sunken Trench and Railway Support. "D" Company moved up close behind "C" Company. Besides this were encountered in 2nd objective in "A" Company's, "B" Coy's. These were several machine gun nests in, and in front of, "B" Company's. These were successfully dealt with. "E" Company moved forward through "A" Company to further trench about X.14.c.5.5. and 2 platoons from left of "B" Company. During this move precisely no opposition was encountered. 2 Platoons of "B" Company passed over their objective in French Trench and eventually reached Sunk Road in X.14.c.5.5. On reaching this point	"A" Coy. Cpt E.T.Welsh. Comdg. 2/Lt G.Taylor " J.S.Willson " A. Cox. "B" Coy. Cpt J.Dawson,MC Comdg 2/Lt W.M. Sweeney. 2/Lt E. Troup. "C" Coy. Lieut J.McVey. Comdg 2/Lt V.W. Manwaring. 2/Lt A. Garman. "D" Coy. Cpt C.W.McConnan. Comdg Lt W.D.Perrins. 2/Lt G.Stansbury " C.H.S.Rand. Cpt N.F.G. Scott, RAMC. Appendix C D(a) D(b)
		5.0 a.m.		

WAR DIARY
or
INTELLIGENCE SUMMARY.
(Erase heading not required.)

Army Form C. 2118.

Place	Date	Hour	Summary of Events and Information	Remarks and references to Appendices
		8.45 a.m.	a Battery of 77 m.m. guns were seen in action and were immediately kept under rifle fire until units of 110th Infantry Brigade passed through and captured the battery complete with teams and personnel. 1 platoon of "A" Company moved from CAVALRY SUPPORT to SUNN ROAD behind the leading platoons of that company. 2 platoons of "B" Coy in CAVALRY SUPPORT moved forward and rejoined remainder of Company. 2 supporting platoons of "C" company moved to CAVALRY SUPPORT, X.19.c.8.3. 110th Brigade moved forward through the line of Battalion, Bn HEADQUARTERS on hill C.13 remaining there, EAST of THRUSH VALLEY, where they were held up by fire from POPLAR TRENCH. Other troops could be seen moving to EAST in A.20.b. and on to BATH LANE, X.21.2. Situation of Division on our right was not clear. PASCHAL SUR Trenches on our Side were occupied by 55th Division, but hostile machine gun fire was still coming from posts in the East and from further South in enemy artillery. The area East of CAVALRY SUPPORT was fairly heavily shelled by enemy artillery.	
		9 a.m.	DURHAM TRENCH was reached on the left with 12/13th N.F., who had reached their objective in CHERRY AVENUE. Information was received that 15th Lincolns had reached their objective on left of 12/13th N.F. in LAUREL TRENCH. 14th Division passed through 50th Division on right, POPLAR TRENCH and CHESTNUT AVENUE still remaining in the enemy's hands. Companies reorganised and consolidated in platoon areas. During the day there was very little increase of hostile artillery. Heavy hostile shelling in vicinity of "B" Company's position, but no infantry action followed.	
		5.30 p.m.	Orders received for reorganisation of Brigade Front. Front to be held by 2nd Lincolns on Right, 12/13th N.F. on Left, with 1st Lincolns in support behind 12/13th N.F.	
		10 p.m.	"A" Coy held with all 4 platoons from junction of BATH and BRAKE ROADS, X.19.c.4.5. to BATH LANE (inclusive) as an outpost line. "B" Coy remained in present position. 16 machine guns also being in this sector.	

D. D. & L., London, E.C.
(A1026) W.W.5300/P713 750,000 2/18 Sch. 82 Forms/C.2118/16.

Army Form C. 2118.

WAR DIARY
or
INTELLIGENCE SUMMARY.
(Erase heading not required.)

Instructions regarding War Diaries and Intelligence Summaries are contained in F.S. Regs., Part II. and the Staff Manual respectively. Title pages will be prepared in manuscript.

Place	Date	Hour	Summary of Events and Information	Remarks and references to Appendices
	1918	3.30 a.m.	"B" Coy handed over their position to the Leicesters and withdrew to CAVALRY SUPPORT from its junction with RAILWAY at X.1.c.4.2. to X.19.a.3.4. "B" Company moved to CAVALRY SUPPORT from left of "B" Coy. with WALK (inclusive). The line held by "A", "C" and "D" Companies was established as the main line of resistance.	
		11 a.m.	Reorganization of line held by Battn complete. 1st Division on right in conjunction with ____ Brigade on left advanced, and more checked by enemy at POPLAR TRENCH.	
		5 p.m.	Enemy put down a intense barrage on the left of Division on our right. This seemed to be coming from "D" Company's area. A little's later no infantry action by the enemy appeared to follow. Battalion was believed by 2 Companies 5th Scottish Rifles. (52nd Div.) 1 company taking over the held by "A" Coy. The other company relieving "C" Company, with 2 platoons each "D" Company with 2 platoons with "C" Companies with 1 platoon each. Relief complete.	
		9.30 p.m.	On relief, Battn moved to billets North of NURTH.	
		10.30 p.m.	In the period 3 a.m. - 10th March, 19th/20th, Battn suffered the following casualties :- 2/Lieut G.H.S. Hunt (1st Northumberland Fus.) attached - Killed. 2/Lieut G. Stansbury - Wounded. 2/Lieut A.V. Mawaring (25th N.F.) attached - Wounded. Other Ranks Killed - 5. Wounded - 59. Missing - 6. The attack on the morning of the 18th was carried out in a heavy storm of rain. On reaching its final objective, the Battn had recaptured the line held by the Brigade on March 21st, 1918. Once again the dash, determination and enthusiasm of all ranks ensured the brilliantly successful results obtained by the Battn, which, since the opening of the offensive on August 21st has consistently added to its record, the rebaking of our old front line coming as the climax.	

Army Form C. 2118.

WAR DIARY
or
INTELLIGENCE SUMMARY.
(Erase heading not required.)

Place	Date	Hour	Summary of Events and Information	Remarks and references to Appendices
W. of MESNIL	20th	2 p.m.	A large number of machine guns were captured during this last advance, and prisoners captured totalled approximately :- 1 Officer and 80 other ranks, chiefly from the 403rd R.I. of the 201st Division. A considerable number of enemy dead were found in the trenches as the result of our bombardment, also a good percentage of wounded. Battn rested in billets north of BUIRE. Later moved to camp West of L'ESNIL-en-ARROUISE (U.5.c.). Route - BUIRE - MERAUCOURT - MESNIL. Battn moved in following order :- Bn H.Q. "D" "B" "A" "C".	Ref 57cS.W. 1/20,000.
	21st	11 a.m.	Battn in Corps Reserve. Nucleus Party joined Battalion. Draft of 1/1 Other Ranks.	
	22nd		Battn still in Corps Reserve. Draft of 96 do	
	23rd		Battn still in Corps Reserve.	
	24th	1.30 a.m.	Battn still in Corps Reserve. Address by Brigadier to Battalion.	
	25th	5 p.m.	Battn still in Corps Reserve. 62nd Infantry Brigade ordered to relieve 50th Infantry Brigade (17th Div) in front line, GUEUDECOURT Sector. 1st Lincolns on right, 12/13th N.F. on left. 2nd Lincolns in support in trench system W.2 and W.3. Battn moved in following order :- Bn H.Q. "C" "B" "A" "D". Route - MESNIL - across country to ENTRECOURT - EQUANCOURT - thence across country W.2.b.b.b. to W.2.d.7.7. to W.2.b. and d. Disposition of companies as follows :- "A" Company in trench W.2.d.9.6. to W.3.c.5.9. "B" Company in trench W.3.a.2.6. to W.3.c.4.8. "C" Company in trench W.3.a.9.9. "D" Company in trench W.2.b.6.6. to W.2.d.7.7. Battn H.Q. at W.2.d.7.7.	Ref.57cS.E. 1/20,000.

Army Form C. 2118.

WAR DIARY
or
INTELLIGENCE SUMMARY.

(Erase heading not required.)

Place	Date	Hour	Summary of Events and Information	Remarks and references to Appendices
W. of GOUZEAUCOURT	26th	9 p.m.	Battalion in position as above. Large number of enemy planes over our lines, but no bombs dropped in Battn area. Night passed off very quietly.	
	27th	5.20 a.m.	Enemy extremely quiet during day, but about 10 p.m. enemy shelled battery positions, a few shells falling near "C" Company. Barrage opened for attack North of our positions. Enemy retaliation to this was slight, a few shells only falling near "C" Company.	
		7.40 a.m.	Barrage opened for attack on our front, 12/13th N.F. attacking AFRICAN TRENCH.	
		9.30 a.m.	12/13th N.F. reported to have gained their objective, but 13th Brigade on left was held up and did not get up in line.	
		10.30 a.m.	"C" Company moved forward 200 yards to valley in Q.34.a. 300 yards behind 12/13th Northumberland Fusiliers, and came under orders of O.C., 12/13th N.F., ready to act as reserve company to that Battalion in case of necessity.	
	28th	1 p.m.	Bn H.Q., "A", "B" and "D" Companies moved up in close support of remainder of Brigade. "A" Company into AFRICAN SUPPORT, Q.35.c.2.6. "B" Company to road, Q.34.a. "C" Company again came under orders of O.C., 2nd Lincolns. "D" Company in trenches, Q.34.d. Battn H.Q. moved to dug-out, Q.34.a.	
		2 p.m.	"C" Company moved up into AFRICAN SUPPORT. These movements of companies were necessary in order to be ready to support the attack of the 12/13th N.F. on trenches West of GOUZEAUCOURT. Companies moved forward to take over area occupied by 12/13th N.F. "B" and "C" Companies - trench 300 yards West of GOUZEAUCOURT. "A" and "D" Companies in AFRICAN TRENCH.	
		9 p.m.	Battn H.Q. to AFRICAN TRENCH. Situation to North and West was not clear, but 12/13th N.F. had had during the afternoon patrols as far as RAILWAY West of GOUZEAUCOURT.	

Army Form C. 2118.

WAR DIARY
or
INTELLIGENCE SUMMARY.
(Erase heading not required.)

Instructions regarding War Diaries and Intelligence Summaries are contained in F. S. Regs., Part II. and the Staff Manual respectively. Title pages will be prepared in manuscript.

Place	Date	Hour	Summary of Events and Information	Remarks and references to Appendices
	29th	12.10 a.m.	Orders received to carry out an attack on GONNELIEU in conjunction with 5th Division on left and 1st Lincolns on right. If successful, the attack was to be exploited 2000 yards further East. Owing to late arrival of orders of this attack, only very short and verbal orders could be issued to companies. Battalion formed up on 400 yards front from RAILWAY between GOUZEAUCOURT STATION and QUARRY to North. "A" Company on the right and "D" Company on the left were in the front line. "B" Company on the right and "C" Company on the left were in the second line.	Appendix E
		3.30 a.m.	The artillery barrage came down on a line running due North and South, 1000 yards East of RAILWAY, at 3.30 a.m. It was found impossible, owing to late arrival of orders, for companies to get to their assembly positions in time to move forward so as to get close up to the barrage. Despite the fact, however, that the companies had to move forward over difficult and unknown country in the dark, and through GOUZEAUCOURT, which was being gas-shelled, they all were able to get fairly close up to the barrage. On getting close to RESERVE LINE TRENCH, 200 yards West of GONNELIEU, heavy machine gun fire was opened by the enemy and the companies were unable to advance any further, and positions were taken up in GREEN SWITCH, 500 yards West of GONNELIEU. 5th Division on left and 1st Lincolns on right were also unable to reach their objectives. During the day there was a considerable amount of sniping coming from trench West of GONNELIEU, and enemy artillery was active just before dusk in vicinity of RAILWAY. "A" Company withdrawn to trenches between GREEN SWITCH and RAILWAY and became the support company	Officers with Battn. at 3.30 a.m. 29th Bn H.Q. Lt.Col E.P. Lloyd, DSO, Commanding. Cpt. J.F.Clingo, M.C. Adjutant. 2/Lt W.E.Beavin Intellige Off. "C" Coy Cpt L.T.Welsh Commanding. 2/Lt J.D.Wilson G. Taylor.
		9 p.m.	4 machine guns, attached to Battalion, were placed in position in GREEN SWITCH. "C" Company were on left, North of GOUZEAUCOURT - CONNELIEU Road, "B" Company in centre and "D" Company on right. Battn H.Q. on RAILWAY behind "A" Company.	

Army Form C. 2118.

WAR DIARY
or
INTELLIGENCE SUMMARY.
(Erase heading not required.)

Instructions regarding War Diaries and Intelligence Summaries are contained in F. S. Regs., Part II. and the Staff Manual respectively. Title pages will be prepared in manuscript.

Place	Date	Hour	Summary of Events and Information	Remarks and references to Appendices
Railway East of GONNELIEU.	30th	4 a.m.	The attack on GONNELIEU was assisted by one tank called "KINTORE", which, however, was knocked out on reaching the enemy's line.	"B" Coy. Lt. J.Lawson, M.C. Command.
		5 a.m.	Enemy quiet during night and patrols sent out towards GONNELIEU found the enemy still holding his line.	2/Lt. E. Troup. 2/Lt. E. Sweeney.
		9 a.m.	Our artillery heavily bombarded GONNELIEU. There was every indication that the enemy had withdrawn from GONNELIEU and patrols sent out from "C" company verified this and were able to occupy RESERVE LINE. "C" Company and "B" Company were ordered to advance North and South of GONNELIEU respectively, and occupy the trenches 300 yards East of the village.	"C" Coy. Lt. T. Hovey. Command. 2/Lt A.C.Garman. 2/Lt E.A.Russell.
		11 a.m.	This was done without opposition. "A" Company on left and "D" Company on right then moved forward through "C" and "B" Companies and occupied SUNK ROAD 1000 yards East of GONNELIEU, between GIMBLER QUARRY and BANTEUX SPUR.	"D" Coy. 2/Lt. O.T.Daniel, M.C. Command. 2/Lt A. Cox.
		1 p.m.	"C" and "B" Companies then moved forward to final objective, 800 yards in front of "A" and "D" Companies. This position commanded St QUENTIN CANAL, 600 yards in valley in front, and also the rising ground on far side on which is the HINDENBURG LINE. The enemy had entirely withdrawn to the East side of the CANAL. Battn H.Q. established in trench at BANTEUX just East of GONNELIEU. At the final objective touch was gained with 7th LEICESTERS on Right and 5th Division on left. 1st Lincolns moved forward over BANTEUX SPUR on to line of CANAL. In the attack on GONNELIEU the following casualties were sustained :-	Cpt W.F.G.Scott, K.A.& C.
		3 p.m.	Officers - NIL. Other ranks. Killed. Wounded. Missing. 10 39 17 It is interesting to note that the Battalion had, in April, 1917, carried out a successful attack on GONNELIEU. On reaching GONNELIEU, several wounded men who were taken prisoners the previous day were found in the dug-outs and taken back.	

WAR DIARY
or
INTELLIGENCE SUMMARY.

Army Form C. 2118.

Since August 21st, 1918, the following awards for gallantry in action have been made to officers, N.C.O's and men of the Battalion:-

BAR TO MILITARY CROSS.

Capt. (Rev.) M. Troop, D.S.O., M.C., A.C.D. Attached.

MILITARY CROSS.

T/Lt. J. Dawson. T/2nd Lt. R. Sharpe. T/2nd Lt. H.M. Irvine.
T/2nd Lt. A. Fairmann.

DISTINGUISHED CONDUCT MEDAL.

51515 Sergt H. Hockley. 41255 Pte (L/C) W. Guy.

MILITARY MEDAL.

236128 Sgt G.E. Hand.	52221 Sgt A.H. Barlow.		32993 Sgt F. Mather.
8122 " W. Child.	6655 " J.W. Rittaway.		44852 " H. Tuddenham.
258144 " H. Evans.	6466 " A. Lilley.		8661 " J. Cutts.
32910 Cpl A. Hillam.	44228 L/c J. Cunniffe.		51514 L/c J.F. Sillis.
49500 Pte G. Walker.	200-29 Pte F. Needham.		49179 Pte H. Booth.
201028 " H.A. Smith.	44952 " G.E. Marmont.		54917 " W. Nickerson.
42285 " W. Gentry.	242546 " F. Nebutt.		54472 " T.A. Cook.
43417 " A.W. Clapham.	15316 " N. Airl.		

E. Lloyd Lt Colonel.
Cmdg. Lincolnshire Regt.

SECRET.   Copy No. 8.

62nd Infantry Brigade Order No. 18.

Ref. Map Sheet
57c S.E. 1/20,000.   16th September 1918.

1.   The enemy is holding the general line CHAPEL HILL, VAUCELLETTE FARM, PEIZIERE, EPEHY, in considerable strength but, it is believed, in little depth.

2. (a)   The Vth Corps is attacking on a date which has been communicated to those concerned and at a Zero Hour which will be notified later, in conjunction with the Fourth Army and other Armies to the South.

    (b)   The 173rd Bde. will be attacking on our right during the first phase of operations, i.e., up to and including capture of POPLAR TRENCH.

    (c)   The 50th Inf Bde and 52nd Inf. Bde. will be attacking on our left and will include FIVES TRENCH in their objective.

3. (a)   The 21st Division will capture successively the BROWN, GREEN and RED lines (See Map).

    (b)   The 62nd Infantry Bde. will capture the BROWN and GREEN Lines.

    (c)   The 110th and 64th Inf. Bdes. will advance close/behind the 62nd Inf. Bde. and pass through the latter Bde., when it has gained the GREEN Line, to a final objective the RED LINE.

4. (a)   The Bde. will be formed up on a taped line running through W.24.a.4.0, W.18.c.5.0, W.18.a.6.0. The foremost troops will be up to this line.

    (b)   A second taped line will be laid 200 yards West of the first. All troops of the Bde. will be formed up inside these two lines by Zero minus 1 hour.

    (c)   Troops detailed for the second objective will advance from their assembly positions 50 yards behind the last line of those detailed for the first objective.

    (d)   Formations and distances between waves and lines will be as already communicated to Battln. Commdrs.

                                                                (e)

- 2 -

(e) The completion of assembly will be notified to Bde. H.Qrs. by the code word "SOUP".

5. The attack and capture of the 1st and 2nd Objectives will be carried out by the 2nd Lincoln R. on the right, 12/13th Northd. Fus. in the centre, and 1st Lincoln R. on the left.

Boundaries and objectives will be as shewn on the attached Map (issued to Battlns., T.M.Bty. and 21st Division only).

After capture of the 1st Objective there will be a pause of 18 minutes, when the troops detailed for the 2nd Objective will form up behind the Railway Embankment running North and South through X.13 and 19, and pass through troops in the 1st Objective.

6. Liaison Posts will be established with neighbouring Units as follows :-

(a) Between 2nd Lincoln R. and 173rd Inf. Bde. at X.19.c.2.0 - X.19.c.4.0 - and X.20.c.2.0.
This last Post will be a joint Post consisting of one Platoon found by each Unit.

(b) Between 1st Lincoln R. and 50th Inf. Bde. at S.E. corner of BIRCH TREE COPSE (X.13.b.3.1).
This Post will be a joint one consisting of one Platoon found by each Units.

7. As soon as Objectives are captured they will be consolidated, and the Bde. will be re-organised as follows :-

12/13th Northd. Fus., will take over the line from the 2nd Lincoln R. to the Southern Divisional Boundary with 2 Coys. in the front line and 2 Coys. in CAVALRY SUPPORT.

1st Lincoln R., will hold the front line from LEITH WALK to the Northern Divisional Boundary with 2 Coys., and will have 1 Coy. in the BROWN LINE West of VAUCELLETTE FARM and one Coy. in Reserve in CAVALRY SUPPORT.

2nd Lincoln R., concentrated in LINNET VALLEY in Divisional Reserve ready to support either of the leading Bdes. This Battln. will be concentrated as soon as 110th Inf. Bde. have passed through them.

8. The O.C. 15th Squadron R.A.F. will be arranging for a contact aeroplane to call for flares as early as possible after daylight and subsequently at odd hours

- 3 -

(i.e. 0 a.m., 9 a.m., 11 a.m. etc.)
RED flares will be used.

Flares will be lit by the foremost troops at the above hours or at any other hour, when called for by the contact aeroplane, sounding a Klaxon Horn.

The aeroplane signal to denote the assembly of enemy to counter-attack is the dropping of a Red Smoke Bomb over the place where the enemy is seen.

9. The following appendices will be issued :-

    Appendix 'A' - Artillery arrangements.
       :   'B' - Administrative arrangements.
       :   'C' - Machine gun arrangements.
       :   'D' - Trench Mortar arrangements.
       :   'E' - Signal arrangements.
       :   'F' - Medical arrangements.

10. (a) Bde. H.Qrs. will open at BRICKYARD, W.21.c.0.0 at 9 p.m. Zero minus 1 day.
Location and opening of Advance Bde. Report Centre will be notified later.

    (b) Battln. H.Qrs. will be established before 11 p.m. on Zero minus 1 day, as follows :-

        12/13th Northd. Fus. - SUNKEN ROAD W.18.c.90.25.
        1st Lincoln R. - Dug-out W.18.c.85.50.
        2nd Lincoln R. - Place to be notified later.

11. Watches will be synchronised at Bde. H.Qrs. W.21.c.0.0 at 9.30 p.m. Zero minus 1 day. Battlns. and T.M.Bty. will each send an Officer to be at Bde. H.Qrs. at that hour.

12. A C K N O W L E D G E .

                                    Captain,
Issued through Signals   Bde. Major,
   at 6.0 p.m.   62nd Infantry Bde.

                                    Distribution page 4.

```
Copy No.  1  -  G. O. C.
          2  -  Bde. Major.
          3  -  Staff Captain.
          4  -  Signals.
          5  -  Bde. Transport Officer.
          6  -  12/13th Northd. Fus.
          7  -  1st Lincoln R.
          8  -  2nd Lincoln R.
          9  -  62nd L. T. M. Bty.
         10  -  'C' Coy. 21st Bn. M.G.C.
         11  -  21st Division.
         12  -  C. R. A.
         13  -  64th Infantry Bde.
         14  -  110th Infantry Bde.
         15  -  50th Infantry Bde.
         16  -  52nd Infantry Bde.
         17  -  173rd Infantry Bde.
         18  -  19th Infantry Bde.
         19  -  65th Field Ambulance.
         20  -  War Diary.
         21  -  File.
         22  -  File.
```

APPENDIX "B" to 62nd Inf. Bde. Order No. 18.

ADMINISTRATIVE ARRANGEMENTS.

1. Ammunition.

    (a) A.R.P. is at V.29.c.0.5.
    (b) Divl. Grenade and S.A.A. Dump is at V.13.c.6.6.; a forward dump is being formed at W.21.b.3.3.

2. Rations.

    Men will go into action carrying rations for Z Day and their Iron Rations. The supply of rations will be normal.

3. Petrol Tins.

    Every effort must be made to send back and salve empty petrol tins. Holes must not be made in the top of petrol tins to facilitate pouring water out of them as this ruins them for further use.

4. Equipment.

    Men will go into action wearing fighting order and carrying 120 rds. S.A.A. Grenades etc. will be carried as directed by Battln. Commdrs.

5. Transport.

    Transport lines will remain in their present positions. A pack train has been organised in the Brigade and M.G. Bn. 'A' Echelon First Line Transport will move under orders of the Brigade Commdr.

6. Casualties.

    Every effort must be made to forward estimated casualties as early as possible. The prompt supply of reinforcements depends entirely on the rendering of these returns.

7. Straggler Posts.

    The A.P.M. will arrange for a line of straggler posts on the NURLU – FINS Road. Straggler collecting posts will be at V.18.c.1.8.
    Each Battln. of 62nd Inf. Bde. will arrange for Regtl. Police to form one Straggler Post in the YELLOW LINE within their Battln. Boundaries.

8. Prisoners of War Cage.

    Prisoners of War Cage will be at V.18.c.1.9. A.P.M. will take over prisoners of war from fighting escorts at this point.

P.T.O.

APPENDIX 'C' to 62nd Inf. Bde. Order No. 18.

MACHINE GUN ARRANGEMENTS.

1. "D" Coy. 21st Battln. and "A" and "C" Coys. 33rd Battln. will support the attack of 62nd Inf. Bde. on to the BROWN LINE by Barrage Fire.

2. On completion of above Barrage, "A" and "C" Coys. 33rd Battln. will remain in Battery positions until further orders.
   "D" Coy. 21st Battln. will move to positions on PEIZIERE RIDGE at X.19.a & c., and will carry out direct overhead fire in support of the attack on the RED LINE.

3. "A" and "B" Coys. 21st Battln. will come under the orders of B.G.C. 110th and 64th Inf. Bdes. respectively for the attack on, and consolidation of the RED LINE.

4. "C" Coy. 21st Battln., less 2 sections, will come under the orders of the B.G.C. 62nd Inf. Bde. for the attack on and consolidation of the BROWN LINE. 8 guns will be placed on VAUCELLETTE FARM SPUR in X.13.c. for direct overhead fire in support of the attack on the RED LINE.
   As soon as the RED LINE is captured or the attack Infantry are consolidating a definite line, those guns will take up defensive positions as follows :-
   2 guns at W.24.d.3.6 firing N.E.
   2 guns at W.18.d.3.9 firing E. and N.E.
   2 guns at W.24.a.8.8 firing E. and S.E.
   2 guns at W.24.b.9.9 firing N.E.

5. The 8 guns of "C" Coy. under the orders of B.G.C. 62nd Inf. Bde. will be allotted as follows :-

   4 guns to advance with the 1st Lincoln R.
   4 guns to advance with the 2nd Lincoln R.

   Section Officers will report to Battln. H.Qrs. under arrangements made by O.C. "C" Coy. 21st M.G.Battln. with O.C. Battln. concerned.

6. The 8 guns of "C" Coy. 21st Battln. on VAUCELLETTE FARM SPUR, and 16 guns of "D" Coy. on PEIZIERE RIDGE must be prepared to support the attack on the RED LINE by indirect methods if found necessary on account of smoke or fog.

7. All forward guns will be used with the utmost boldness, and every opportunity taken of ground from which direct overhead fire can support the attack.

*****

APPENDIX 'F' to 62nd Inf. Bde. Order No. 18.

MEDICAL ARRANGEMENTS.

1. Main Dressing Station - P.32.central.

    Corps Walking Wounded Station - V.2.central.

    A combined A.D.S. will be formed in the 38th Div. Area on the FINS - EQUANCOURT Road at V.11.a.2.2.

2. O.C. 65th Field Ambulance will be responsible for the clearance of the line from 9 p.m. 17th and will relieve 19th Field Ambulance at Advanced Car Post at W.14.b.4.3.

    Reserve bearers of 63rd, 64th and 65th Field Ambulances will assemble in the line of dug-outs at W.14.b.

****

APPENDIX 'G' to 62nd Inf. Bde. Order No. 18.

MISCELLANEOUS.

1. Anti-Tank Minefield.

    The C.R.E. will detail parties of R.E. to accompany 62nd Inf. Bde. As soon as the GREEN LINE is captured these parties will start making gaps and improving existing gaps in the minefield. Gaps will be marked with a notice board on each side marked thus :-

2. Captured Artillery.

    The position of any guns that may be captured at which there are ammunition dumps will be reported to Bde. H.Q. who will at once inform the affiliated Artillery Bde. Commdr. so that Medium Trench Mortar personnel may be sent forward to serve the guns.

3. Secrecy.

    Attention is drawn to the absolute necessity of preserving secrecy regarding the operations. The probability of the enemy having listening sets in position must be counted upon. Telephone conversation in front of Bde. H.Qrs. will be cut down to a minimum from the time at which the 62nd Inf. Bde. take over the line. Under no circumstances will any reference to made to forthcoming operations on the telephone.

4. Intelligence.

    All maps, papers, documents and pay books will be collected by Battlns. from enemy dead and forwarded to Bde. H.Qrs.

    Identity discs will be left on the dead.

    Papers will not be collected from prisoners.

    All documents found in dug-outs will be forwarded to Bde. H.Qrs.

    Battlns. will wire (priority) to Bde. H.Qrs. the Regts. and, if possible, the Divisions, to which the first batch of prisoners belong, and will subsequently wire any new identification.

    All prisoners will be sent to Bde. H.Qrs. W.21.c.0.0.

    It is very important that escorts bringing down prisoners should know approximately the time and place of capture.

APPENDIX 'D' to 62nd Inf. Bde. Order No. 18.

TRENCH MORTAR ARRANGEMENTS.

1. The 62nd L.T.M.Bty. and the 19th L.T.M.Bty., acting under orders of O.C., 62nd L.T.M.Bty, will co-operate in the operations as follows :-

    13 guns will be used for barrage.
    1 mobile gun attached to 1st Lincoln R.
    1   :   :   :   : 2nd Lincoln R.

    These mobile guns will report to Battalions on the latters' arrival at their new H.Qrs. on Y/Z night.

2. The guns used for barrage work will conform with the artillery barrage tables already issued.

3. After the barrage is completed the 5 guns of the 62nd L.T.M.Bty. and the 8 guns of the 19th L.T.M.Bty. will be withdrawn to Bde. H.Qrs. (W.21.c.0.0) under orders to be issued by O.C., 62nd L.T.M.Bty.

****

APPENDIX 'E' to 62nd Inf. Bde. Order No. 18.

COMMUNICATIONS.

1. The following methods will be used :-

    Runners.
    Visual.
    Telephone.
    Wireless.

2. Brigade H.Qrs.   -   W.21.c.0.0.
    Adv. Bde. Report Centre -   W.23.b.5.0.

    A line will be run via 2nd Lincoln R. H.Qrs. at W.23.b.5.0 to 12/13th Northd. Fus. H.Qrs. in Sunken Road W.18.c.90.25, and then to 1st Lincoln R. H.Qrs. dug-out W.18.c.85.50.

3. Visual.

    1st Lincoln R. will establish a visual station at their Headquarters.

    Location of Bde. Visual Station - Bde. H.Qrs.

4. Wireless.

    Flank Bdes. and following forward co-ordinates :-

    W.23.a.3.5.
    W.18.c.85.50.

5. Brigade Runner Post will be established at Adv. Brigade Report Centre.

******

SUMMARY OF PRISONERS ETC.

Taken by British Army from August 1st to 29th :-

    57,318 prisoners (including 1,283 Officers).

    657 Guns (including 153 heavy guns).

    5,750 Machine Guns.

    Over 1,000 Trench Mortars.

Taken by Third Army from August 21st to September 2nd :-

    596 Officers, 20015 Other Ranks.

    138 Guns.

Taken by Vth Corps from August 21st to September 2nd :-

    111 Officers, 4,709 Other Ranks.

Taken by 21st Division from August 21st to September 2nd :-

    45 Officers, 1,242 Other Ranks.

    12 Guns.

The average depth of the advance is 12 miles.

APPENDIX 'A' to 62nd Infantry Brigade
Order No. 18.

1. The attack of the 62nd Infantry Brigade is being supported by the 94th, 72nd and 315th Bdes. R.F.A.

2. Full details as to Creeping Barrage are given on attached Map "B". (only issued to Battlns).

3. Intensified rate of fire will be opened when the Barrage starts to creep forward again after halting in front of the 1st Objective.

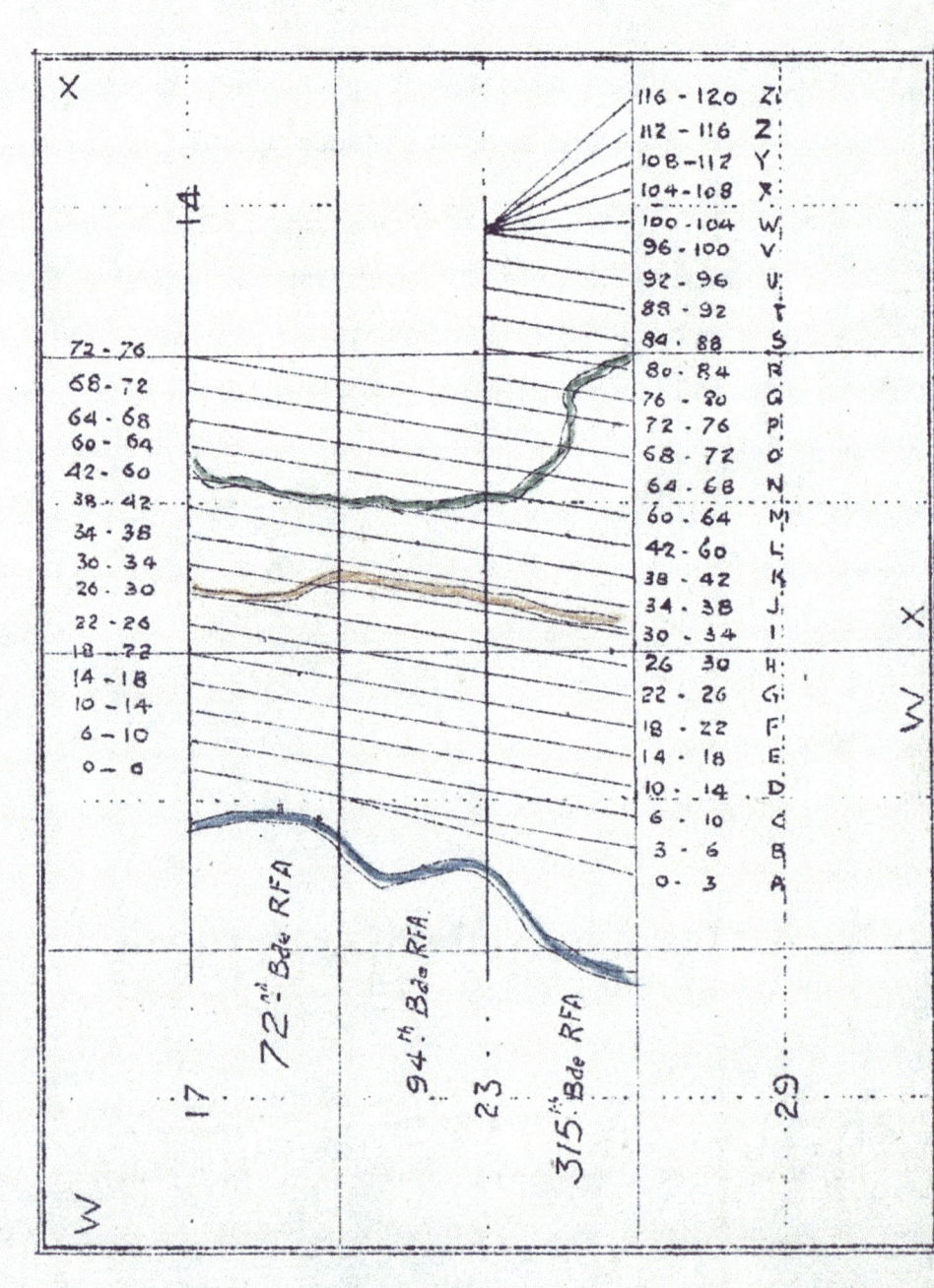

Barrage Map issued with 21 D.A.O.O No. 5

First Operation

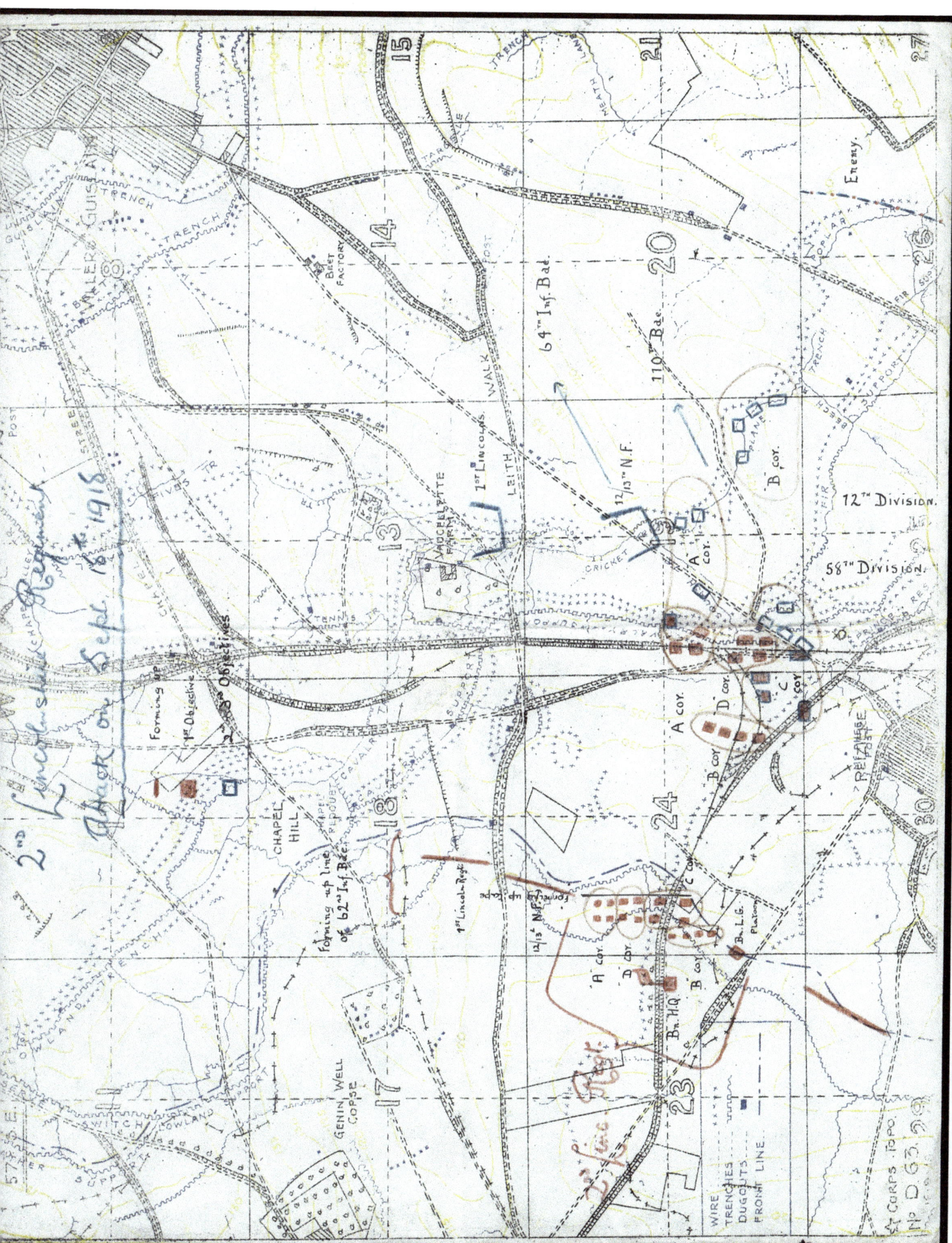

2nd Lincolnshire Regiment - Attack on Sept. 18th 1918.

Appendix B

MESSAGE FORM.

.... DIVISION.

MAP REFERENCE OR MARK
ON MAP AT BACK.

1. I am at _____ and am consolidating.
2. I am at _____ and have consolidated.
3. I am at _____
4. Am held up by M.G. at _____
5. I need:
   - Ammunition.
   - Bombs.
   - Rifle Grenades.
   - Water.
   - Very Lights.
   - Stokes Shells.
6. Counter-attack forming up at _____ on Right at _____ on Left
7. I am in touch with _____ on Right.
8. I am not in touch on Left.
9. Am being shelled from _____
10. I estimate my present strength at _____ rifles.
11. Hostile { Battery / Machine Gun / Trench Mortar } active at _____

Time _____ m.   Name _____
                            Platoon _____

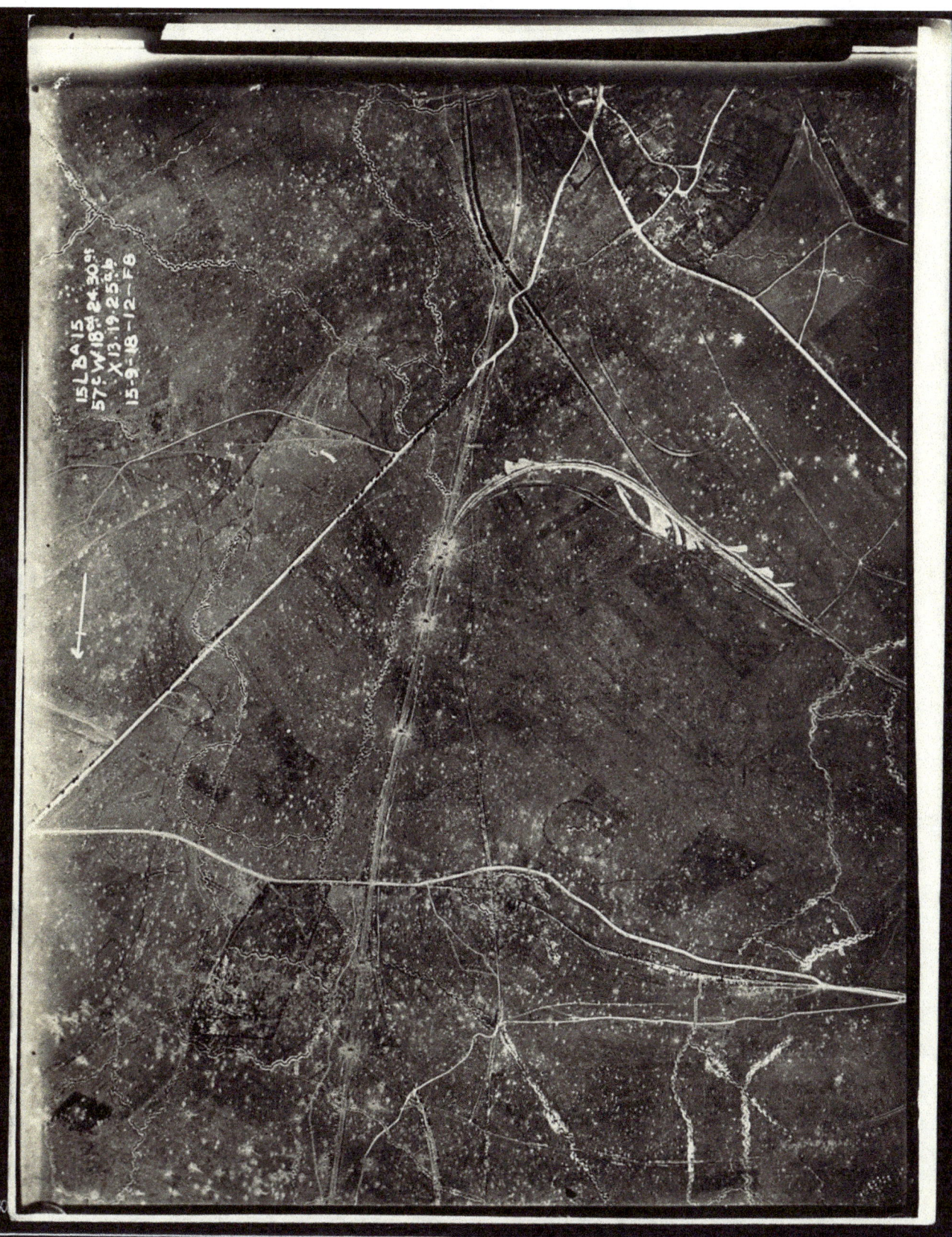

WO 95/2155

Appendix D (6)

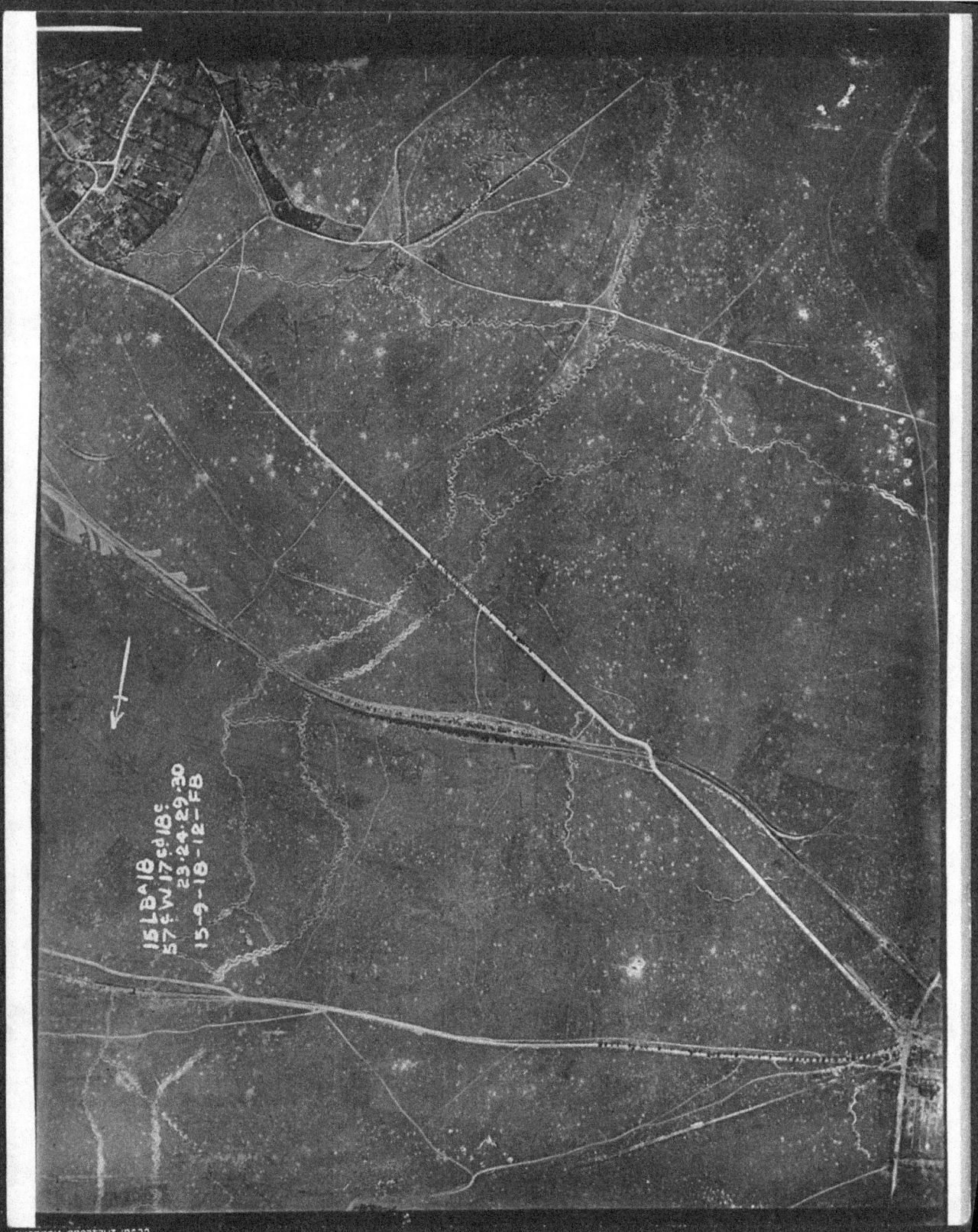

WO 95/2154

Appendix D (a)

Appendix E

MESSAGE FORM.

TO .... No. ....

1.—I am at ....
   NOTE.—Either give map reference or mark your position by a X on a map or trace.

2.—My Line runs ....

3.—My Platoon/Company is at .... and is consolidating.

4.—My Platoon/Company is at .... and has consolidated.

5.—Am held up (a) by wire at ....
   (b) at .... by M.G. at ....

6.—Enemy holding strong point ....

7.—I am in touch with .... on Right at ....
                                              Left at ....

8.—I am not in touch with .... on Right at ....
                                                  Left at ....

9.—Am in need of ....

10.—Counter attack forming at ....

11.—I estimate my present strength at .... rifles.

12.—Add any other useful information here :—

Time .... m.   Name ....
Date ....1918.   Platoon ....
                                       Company ....
                                       Battalion ....

(a) Carry no maps or papers which may be of value to the enemy.
(b) Give no information if captured, except the following, which you are bound to give :—
    Name and Rank.
(c) Collect all captured maps and papers and send them in at once.

Confidential.

War Diary
of
2nd Battalion
The Lincolnshire Regiment
from - 1st October 1918.
to - 31st October 1918.

WAR DIARY or INTELLIGENCE SUMMARY

Army Form C. 2118.

(Erase heading not required.)

Place	Date	Hour	Summary of Events and Information	Remarks and references to Appendices
E. of GONNELIEU	1st		Battn. remained in positions taken up on previous day as follows: "B" + "C" Coys on front line, RIBBLE TRENCH, R34 6+d, "A" Coy extending N. of BANTEUX ROAD and "D" Coys on REAR TRENCH – GLASGOW TRENCH R28-34. Battn Q.M. TRENCH E. of GONNELIEU R29 d.5.5.	Ref Sh 57° SE 1/20,000
		5 p.m.	2 platoons of "B" + "C" Coys withdrawn today – outs behind so as to enable the men to get as much rest as possible	
			Enemy exceptionally quiet during whole 24 hours	
E. of GONNELIEU	2nd	3 p.m.	Heavy shelling of area occupied by 10 Coy. GONNELIEU was also shelled during day. Shelling of area in front of Bn H.Q. also was for Gas Shells.	2/Lt BROOM rejoined
E. of GONNELIEU	3rd	10 a.m.	Enemy shelled area E of GONNELIEU, but otherwise very quiet during day	
		9 p.m.	62nd Div Bde relieved by 110th Bde. 2nd Leicesters relieved by 1st Leicesters and they marched to Billets v/g of BOISSACOURT At B Coys in area Q34 C, C & D Coys in area Q34 G+d, Bn Hd Q^rs Q34 a.3. Route GONNELIEU – GOUZEAUCOURT – FINS road.	
		6.30 pm	Relief Complete. No shelling of Battalion on relief + no casualties	
Q34 a 4.5	4th		Batt. at Rest in Bon Heures	
	5th		Batt. still in Bon Heures	
		5 pm	Brigade ordered to move forward to attack on Cambrai with Bn+ no detail, who had moved forward in small during day, 2nd Leicesters moved to trenches E of GONNELIEU ranked 2 days previously A Coy SUNKEN ROAD T26.34 B Coy TURNER QUARRY R30 d 9.9 C Coy GLASGOW TRENCH R34 c D Coy CHESHIRE QUARRY R34 a	

WAR DIARY
or
INTELLIGENCE SUMMARY.

(Erase heading not required.)

Army Form C. 2118.

Place	Date	Hour	Summary of Events and Information	Remarks and references to Appendices
R.33.c.8.6	5th	9 p.m.	Bn Hd Qrs KITCHEN QUARRY R.33.C.8.6.	
do	6th		Companies in positions as above.	
	7th	2 p.m.	Companies remain in above positions.	
		10 p.m.	Battn. moved forward to positions E. of ST QUENTIN CANAL S.2.n.3.	Ref 57 b.S.W.
			Battn. moved forward to NUROY LINE S3.6. & d. taking up positions prior to attack from right to right	1/20,000
			as follows:— D—B—C—A Bn. Hd. Qr. in S.5.d.9.5.	
		12 M/N	Whole of Battalion in positions in NUROY LINE.	
35.6.9.5	8th	11.00	Barrage opened for attack by 6th Bde. on BEAUREVOIR LINE.	
		05.30	Barrage opened for attack and "A" Bde on BEAUREVOIR LINE	
		05.55	A Coy moved forward to [...] up the barricade by pill box to make its front	
			by "D" + "B"+C Coys. Coys formed up in 2 waves. A Coy on right + 10 Coy on left of NUROY ROAD N.32.C followed by 2nd waves of 5 mins	
			and 13 on their left. C Coy on left of 10 + 10 Coy on left of "A" Coy + C	
			[...] of each was 6 + touns jumped forward by not fds to make its [...]	
			in Pill Box N.32. C.14.	
	07.16		A + D Coys moved forward nearly to attack followed later by B+C Coys. 2nd & 3rd moved to BEAUREVOIR LINE close up to Barrage 2 which crossed N.E. central.	following officers went forward with attack 8/10/18
		08.00	Barrage opened + battalion moved forward in extended order. by A Coys on order to get lost. Unable to advance forward owing to M.G. fire from right flank the middle of the	
			38th Div. not being up on his right. A + D Coys pushed forward by the M.G. fire on right + 36th Div on right. At "D" Coys	
		09.00	"B" Coy Commenced digging in N.W. of AMBRE WOOD. But were unable to advance any further owing this part of the [...] and E of CHATEAU N.33.C. "C" Coy moved up in rear of A + "D" Coys. W Coy	
			Coy 6 [...] from N [...] which would reach was not gained until 35.10 on night.	Cox
			shortly from the night attack to the left Brigade who had on to QUARRIES LI.	2/Lt [...]
			returned the [...] [...] [...] position [...]	[...]
			[...] [...] [...] [...] owing to the number of [...]	3rd [...]

Army Form C. 2118.

WAR DIARY
or
INTELLIGENCE SUMMARY.
(Erase heading not required.)

Instructions regarding War Diaries and Intelligence Summaries are contained in F.S. Regs., Part II. and the Staff Manual respectively. Title pages will be prepared in manuscript.

Place	Date	Hour	Summary of Events and Information	Remarks and references to Appendices
			which concealed a large number of the enemy including several Snipers which severely hampered the advance.	B Coy Capt Gambell County 2/Lt Agara 3/Lt Allen MGM
		10.00	1 Section of MG attached to Battn moved up to protect left flank.	
		16.00	B & D Coys ordered to send out patrols to find out enemy dispositions on the ground along enemy's front from WARINCOURT to WG WARINCOURT and Sunken Road WG WARINCOURT N30d. A number of Coys on right "B" Coy on the extreme left had Sunken Road at N3a (covered by patrols going forward to protect right flank) away to N31a and having moved forward.	C Coy Capt Elliot County 2/Lt Nay 2/Lt Chapman 10 Coy Capt Richards M.S County
		18.00	Except for a little MG fire from WARINCOURT itself was very slight opposition and no decisive resistance during this phase of advance, owing to this fact a survey of report as to dispositions of the two leading Coys. The Survey E while conducted for a while was allowed to run out. The leading Coys had not establish survey beyond + B+C Coys advanced + passed through A + D Coys gradually taking up positions along road and front of MILL WOOD N29-30. The forward movement was stopped W of WARINCOURT + did not get beyond at this stage.	2/Lt B[room] 2/Lt O'Donnell MC 2/Lt A WATSON
			On Westward moving reconnaissance of the [...] that moved up close support to the Battalion. I crossed at a hill running S of WARINCOURT. B+C Coys encountered a battn of Infantry who were moving up to attack and were only one casualty was sustained. On the ground to the front WG AVATE WOOD N30 9.6. The 36 [...] on NW from [...] to a [...] in the morning.	
		20.00	Touch gained with [...] N37B5 N by right coy along road N29d + left York and and up to Sunken Road on N31c + N31d in the morning. The enemy retaliation [...] all along our fronts a few shells falling in WARINCOURT WOOD [...] casualties were a few.	

Army Form C. 2118.

WAR DIARY
or
INTELLIGENCE SUMMARY.
(Erase heading not required.)

Place	Date	Hour	Summary of Events and Information	Remarks and references to Appendices
N.33.a.9.6.	1st	20.00	The Enemy heavily shelled area occupied by Battalion with both H.E & Gas during night. Patrols sent out from B & C Coys to reconnoitre village & reported it free from enemy, but companies did not move from their positions, Patrolling being kept up during night. During this advance the tasks of mopping up the various woods was allotted to "A" Coy. Coy. Commander who did their work splendidly. The spirit of the men being good though not considering the difficulties encountered. Casualties are as follows:- Missing 6. Wounded 14. Killed 4. The attack the numbers and energy & fight evinced by the Enemy were but in spite of this fact they again showed great dash and enthusiasm which ensured the success of the day's operations. Runners teams... this attack amounted to approx 60 O.R. and a number of M.G's were taken as well as 2 field Guns already mentioned. Battalion was in touch throughout the operations of a unit went hard to mutual advantage and a unit joined up by the Battalion.	
			Col. Russell H. Wounded 2/Lt OT Donald MC Wounded 2/Lt Ev. Duncy do G.Roan J.S Killed 1 hr	
	2nd	05.30	1/4 Bur passed through to further objectives	
		10.00	Bn. HQ. OK moved up to WANCOURT	
			Whole of Battalion was relieved by 1/5 K.O.S.B. at WANCOURT became Corps Reserve.	

KILLED 14 WOUNDED 70 MISSING 9 TOTAL 93

WAR DIARY or INTELLIGENCE SUMMARY

Army Form C. 2118.

Place	Date	Hour	Summary of Events and Information	Remarks and references to Appendices
Noeux les Mines	10th	16.00	Battn still in (?) billets	
	11th		Nucleus party rejoined Battalion	
Wanquetin	12th		Battn still in Wanquetin billets	
"	13th		do	
"	14th	09.30	Church parade	
"	15th	09.00	Training bombing raid of B&C Companies to Battn. H.Q.s of	
"	16th		Training Continued	
"	17th		do	
"	18th		do	
"	19th	09.45 to 15.00	Practice advance guards area M18-N17 to A Coys infant div	
"		15.00	B&C Coy in support	
"		15.20	2nd Lieut (?) (Regtl) (?) Coy. 2.6.6 and 7th B. result Coy 3 goals 6&7TMB nil. Capt JP Clayg (wounded)	Capt A Harvey took over duties of Adjutant
"	20th	09.00	Church Parade	
"	21st		Battn went on Corps reserve	
"	22nd		2nd Brigade ordered to move forward to INCHY area preparatory to attack on the following morning	
"		10.55	Battn moved off on following order HQ A-B-C-D north WALINCOURT-SELVIGNY-CAULLERY-LIGNY	R4.MAP 57 B NE 1/20,000
		14.15	CAULERY-INCHY	
			B Coy in Billets in INCHY	
			A and C Coys in Caves B.T.D in expressed (?) Bn. HQ O'Brien Bros JOIR	
INCHY		02.40	Battn moved forward to reached attack on enemy positions NE of NEWVILLY south INCHY	
	23rd	04.30	Battn rested on SUNKEN ROAD XJO for breakfast	

WAR DIARY or INTELLIGENCE SUMMARY.

Army Form C. 2118.

Place	Date	Hour	Summary of Events and Information	Remarks and references to Appendices
	23.4.17	05.00	Btn'l'y Bangalore attacked in extended formation from East of OVILLERS + going eastwards on HARPIES RIVER & advance to continue the advance.	Lt Col Adamson Wounded Mentioned 2.1.40 21.10.18
		06.30	There was a little shelling on road but both were resting.	BH Ml Q M
		05.45	Coys made road up to assembly point, rear of Bn'l'y AMERVAL	Lt Col E Lloyd DSO Comdg
			D Coy on the L of A + C in support, B Bn'l'y left supp'e of Coy in 1st supp'd	Capt G Henry acting Adjt
			A + M Q's were up on centre behind C Coy	2/Lt W.E. Deavin I O
		07.30	HQ Coy moved off in order to reach Unit told of 6.11. H.Q. by 07.40 but + had 2 offr +	Lt Stewart L.B.O.
			Companies moving up + reached at a distance of 300 yards.	Capt Joyce S.O
			Soon after, Capt ... ordered to small villages though village. So soon as men had	Capt Scott R.A.M.C.
			left the Batn driven out on a B Coy. Nr top ... considerable amount of shelling	A Coy
			& encountered enemy firstly from high ground but ... were not so heavy as	Capt Richards
			usual.	Lt Perkins
			When the platoons started advancing there was any heavy m.g. fire nor had considerable	2/Lt Chard
			interfered with the direction and consequently by the morning forward more than	B Coy
		10.00	reached their objective and encountered the 23rd Gunfire	Capt Dawson A.C.
			The mist was a good deal + this enabled direction to be re-established the advance	2/Lt Byron
			consisted of orders considered H.Q. K.S.L.I. and heavy shelling came amongst	2/Lt Linsay MC
			on the high ground about ... and there was a new HQ + F.12.67 Fig A.C.	C Coy
		14.00	Batn HQ was established at F.13.G.M.1.3	2/Lt Lingard
		15.00	The general lines F.2.d.4/3 – F.9 central made no good end and we	2/Lt Chapman
			The two supporting Coys are to go through B & C Coys and continue the advance	2/Lt Livesey
		16.00	The advance was soon commenced but the shelling became very heavy + the	D Coy
			enemy made a general counter attack relieved on that position came also	Capt McClamman
			...	2/Lt Kincade
			...	2/Lt Taylor
		17.30	The Coys could have negotiated for the day when the rear elements	Capt McClamman Wounded
			N.W. + S.E. ... F.8 + F.9 etc.	2/Lt Kincade Wounded
				2/Lt Kincade Killed
				2/Lt Livesey Wounded
				2/Lt R H Taylor Wounded

Army Form C. 2118.

WAR DIARY
or
INTELLIGENCE SUMMARY.
(Erase heading not required.)

Instructions regarding War Diaries and Intelligence Summaries are contained in F. S. Regs., Part II. and the Staff Manual respectively. Title pages will be prepared in manuscript.

Place	Date	Hour	Summary of Events and Information	Remarks and references to Appendices
	24.10.18	10.00	15th A. Bn. 10 O.R. & 9th Battn. K.O.Y.L.I. went through to the Battn. to put on forward advance	Ref. Map S/A S.E.
		14.30	The Battn. moved off took up new formations Coy. A on X.27.d.3.4.	
			A Coy advance tanks in X.27.c (North of River)	
			B Coy about X.27. b.1, U.C. in road about X.27.b.20	
			The Battn. was in this order	
	27.10.18	14.30	The Battn. was relieved by 1st Battn. West Ryd. Regt marched to billets over to Wellington	Col. Rd Lloyd DSO 2/Lt W.B. Davin Wounded Sick
	29.10.18		Battn. ordered to return & Bivouac Buss Vp. Huts.	
		12.00	Entrained & proceeded overland reaching French Town nord	A. Coy 2/Lt Chard Coy Comdy
		16.00	Arrived at Railway embankment at point S/A S.E. X.8.y.o and had hot meal	2/Lt Taylor Perkins
		18.00	Moved off in following order B.D.O.A. Coys and allied Ranks Hus Coys taking up following positions	B Coy Lt Dawson M.C. 2/Lt Archer M.C. 2/Lt Lindsay " Jarvis
			A Coy in Support at B Coy Huns (Bket S/A S.E. X.7. A 5.5	C Coy Lt McVay 2/Lt Seymour " Hursten
			B Coy 2 Platoons in SUNKEN ROAD X.11 a.8.6	
			" Advance Platoon X.11.a.0.10	D Coy Capt Walsh 2/Lt Watson
			" Supporting Platoon X.11.c.8.9	Batt Qrs
			C Coy 3 Platoons in Sunken Road X.17.6	Maj Dawson M.C. Capt Montgomery
			" Advance Platoon X.11.b.5.6	Capt Scott Rankin Lt Stewart So
			10 Coy in Sunken Road at Skull S/A S.E. X.11.c (2 Platoons)	2/Lt Joyce Sig Offr
			" Advance Platoon at X.10.d.7	2/Lt Russell T.O.
			" Supporting Platoon at X.11.c.4.2	
			A Bn. H Qrs. at X.31.d.8.6.	
	30.10.18		Heavy Shelling during night but no casualties	
			Enemy shelled Battn. front posts and back area 5,6,7 & 8	
			(Change) in command did advances as follows	

Army Form C. 2118.

WAR DIARY
or
INTELLIGENCE SUMMARY.
(Erase heading not required.)

Instructions regarding War Diaries and Intelligence Summaries are contained in F. S. Regs., Part II and the Staff Manual respectively. Title pages will be prepared in manuscript.

Place	Date	Hour	Summary of Events and Information	Remarks and references to Appendices
	30.10.16		A Coy in support with five Platoons in Trench x.17 a 2.1 to x.17 6.3.3 and two Platoons in Trench x.17 a 5.6 to x.17 a.2.3. Coy Hd Qrs R. Hg. Farm x.17 a.	
			B Coy moved and took up following disposition	
			2 Platoons at Shell St. A.S.E. x.10.0.8.4 to x.11.c.2.2	
			2 Platoons at " x.11.c.4.3 to x.17.a.5.6	
			Coy Hd Qrs in farm x.17 a	
			C Coy 2 Platoons in Sunken Road Sh 51.A.S.E. x.17 b.9 to x.17 b.6.3	
			2 Platoons Platoon x.17 b.5.6 this Platoon supplied a post consisting of one section at x.17 b.8.8.	
			Coy Hd Qrs at Farm x.17 a.	
			D Coy dispositions as follows Sh 51.A.S.E.	
			3 Platoons Sunken Road at x.11.a to x.11.a.9.1 and one Platoon in x.11.D.5.5.	
	31.10.16	03.30	Barrage laid down on enemy positions in conjunction with a raid on enemy side by C/6 flank Bn Enemy came to barrage on Battalion front in strength expected the Battalion intervals throughout the day.	

CASUALTIES 23.10.16 O. RANKS

KILLED	WOUNDED	MISSING	TOTAL
28	132	13	173

[signature] before
Henry Evan [illegible]

War Diary

62nd Bde
21 Div

1st Bn.

Lincolnshire Regt.

November 1918

SECRET.
Confidential.

War Diary Volume 11

of the

2nd Bn Lincolnshire Regiment

for period

1st November 1918

to

30th November 1918.

E. W. Royd Lieut Colonel
Commdg. 2nd Bn Lincolnshire Regt.

Army Form C. 2118.

WAR DIARY
or
INTELLIGENCE SUMMARY.
(Erase heading not required.)

Instructions regarding War Diaries and Intelligence Summaries are contained in F. S. Regs., Part II. and the Staff Manual respectively. Title pages will be prepared in manuscript.

Place	Date	Hour	Summary of Events and Information	Remarks and references to Appendices
Poix du Nord	1.11.18	08-00	Situation unchanged	Ref 51a S.E. 1/20,000
		12-00	Gd GAY Farm and Pt GAY Farm shelled, principally Gas Shelling.	2/Lt Perkins wounded
		17-00	Situation quiet.	
		21-00	Renewed shelling on Gd GAY Farm and Pt GAY Farm (X.17.a.&b.) "A" & "C" Coys began to dig assembly positions along the sunken road in X.17.b.&.d.	
do	2.11.18	02-00	Assembly positions completed, situation quiet.	Ref 57 B 1/40,000
		12-00	Enemy shelled POIX du NORD (F.3.&.4.)	
		15-00	Enemy shelled heavily areas X.17.a.b.&.c. X.21.b.&.d. and X.22.a.&.c.	
		15-30	Our Artillery replied with a heavy bombardment on enemy positions.	
		19-00	62nd Inf Bde relieved by 51st Inf Bde.	
		21-00	Relief complete.	Ref 57 B 1/40,000
VENDEGIES au BOIS	do	22-30	Battalion moved into billets in VENDEGIES-au-BOIS.. area F.13.a. There were no casualties during relief.	
(F.7.8.&13.)	3-11-18		Battalion rested and prepared to move into action on the following day.	2/Lt Broom (Hosp)
do	4-11-18	13-00	62nd Inf Bde, ordered to move up to "B" concentration area X.29.d. in order to be able to follow up the 17th Division who had commenced a frontal attack on the Forest de Mormal at 05-00 hours.	Ref 51 A 1/40,000. Bn Hd qrs
Les TUILERIES		15-00	Battalion arrived at concentration area and rested, h ot was issued.	Maj Goater C.S.O (Comg) M.C.
		15-45	62nd Inf Bde ordered to move up into "B" contentration area S.14.15.& 16.	Capt Dawson M.C.
		18-30	Battalion reached area "B" and rested in S.15.c.	Capt A. Harvey Adjt
		22-00	In order to assist the advance of the 1st Bn Lincolnshire Regt, on the following day, 2 Coys, 2nd Bn Lincolnshire Regt were ordered to make good the thick wood on N.E. side of road ROUTH COULON in T.13.a.&.b. and thus clear up a somewhat obscure situation.	Capt Scott M.C. Lt T.B. Stewart (L.G.O.)
FOREST de MORMAL		23-15	Forward Battn Hd Qrs and A. & B. Coys reached road junction in S.12.c. Battn Hd Qrs established there.	2/Lt H. Joyce S.O. 2/Lt E. Russell IO Ref 51 B S.W. 1/20,000

Army Form C. 2118.

WAR DIARY
or
INTELLIGENCE SUMMARY.
(Erase heading not required.)

Instructions regarding War Diaries and Intelligence Summaries are contained in F. S. Regs., Part II. and the Staff Manual respectively. Title pages will be prepared in manuscript.

Place	Date	Hour	Summary of Events and Information	Remarks and references to Appendices
FORET de MORAL		23-30	"A" Company (less one platoon in reserve at S.12.c.4.5.) advanced down ROUTE COULON and took up positions.	2/Lt Taylor Comdg A. Coy
			Coy Hd Qrs ...... S.18.b.5.8.	B. Coy
			One platoon ...... T.13.a.2.3.	Lt J. Dawson M.C.
			One Platoon ...... T.13.c.9.6.	Comg
			One Platoon ...... T.13.d.6.0.	Ref 51 S.W. 1/20,000
		23-55	"B" Company (less one platoon in reserve at S.12.c.3.4.) moved off and established positions.	C. Coy.
			Coy Hd Qrs ...... S.18.b.5.8.	Lt McVey Comg.
			One Platoon ...... T.13.a.65.80.	D. Coy.
			One Platoon ...... T.13.b.3.4.	Capt S. Wilson
			One Platoon ...... T.13.d.80.35.	Comg.
	5.11.18	01-00	"B" Company in position on N.E. boarder of wood.	
		03-00	Patrols sent out by "B" Coy S.W. down the rides to A. Coy, captured the wood taking 12 prisoners & 4.M.G's The capture of this wood was of great importance.	
		05-00	62nd Inf Bde continues the advance made by the 17th Division. 12/ 13th Bn Northumberland Fusiliers on left. 1st Battn Lincolnshire Regt on right and 2nd Battn Lincolnshire Regt in support. 1st Battn Lincolnshire Regt passed through A. & B. Coys.	
		06-00	Remainder of Battn moved up to A. & B. Coys.	
		08-00	Following the advance, Battalion moved down ROUTE COULON along the CARREFOUR de la TAPPERIE to la TETE NOIRE and rested.	
la TETE NOIRE BERLAIMONT		10-30	Advance continued and Battalion moved to the WESTERN edge of BERLAIMONT when it came under direct M.G. fire from N.E. It was raining hard.	
		12-30	Battalion halted and took up support positions, as the enemy was offering a stiff resistance in the eastern edge of BERLAIMONT, on the bank of the river SAMBRE. Battalion Head Qrs in Farm at U.20.c.8.2.	

Army Form C. 2118.

WAR DIARY
or
INTELLIGENCE SUMMARY.
(Erase heading not required.)

Instructions regarding War Diaries and Intelligence Summaries are contained in F.S. Regs., Part II. and the Staff Manual respectively. Title pages will be prepared in manuscript.

Place	Date	Hour	Summary of Events and Information	Remarks and references to Appendices
BERL AIMONT	5.11.18		A.B.& C.Coys. along Railway embankment running through U.19.& 26.	
		15-00	"D" Company in sunken Road in U.19.d. Protection was established by flank guards and H.Q. Lewis Guns guarded the front.	
		17-00	Enemy shelled continuously BERL AIMONT - TETE NOIRE road in U.19.a & U.20.c.	
		19-00	BERL AIMONT heavily shelled.	
	6-11-18	06-00	Situation quiet but occasional artillery activity.	
		08-00	110th Inf Bde passed through and continued the advance	
		12-00	62nd Inf Bde in support. Battn moved into billets in U.20.c.	
		15-30	Battn Hqrs at U.20.c.9.7.	
		18-00	Enemy shelled BERL AIMONT continuously.	
		18-15	Battn attached to 110th Inf Bde. "D" Company ordered to move to AYMERIES which had already been surrounded and to clear it of any enemy. AYMERIES heavily shelled.	
		21-00	"D" Coy return and report no Enemy in AYMERIES.	
	7-11-18.	09-00	Battn detached from 110th Brigade.	
AYMERIES.	8.11.18	12-00	Battn moves forward to AYMERIES and is billeted there.	
			Battn rested, although the operations carried out by the Battalion were not serious with regard to fighting, the very bad conditions of weather and ground called for considerable endurance on the part of the men.	
	9-11-18		Battn still rested.	
	10.11.18	14-00	Nucleus party rejoined Battalion, Battalion reinforced by 2 Officers and 150 Other ranks.	Ref 51. 1/40,000
	11-11-18	08-30	Received news that hostilities would cease at 11-00 hours, this caused considerable excitement.	
		11-00	Hostilities ceased.	

Army Form C. 2118.

WAR DIARY
or
INTELLIGENCE SUMMARY.
(Erase heading not required.)

Instructions regarding War Diaries and Intelligence Summaries are contained in F. S. Regs., Part II. and the Staff Manual respectively. Title pages will be prepared in manuscript.

Place	Date	Hour	Summary of Events and Information	Remarks and references to Appendices
BACHANT	12.11.18	11.00	2nd Infantry Brigade moved to billets in BACHANT, U.18.& 13.	2/Lt G. Stock in Joined Bn
	13.11.18	09.00	General Inspection Parades.	Maj Richards M.C
	14.11.18	09.00	Battalion carried out Salvage work in area U.17.& 18.	
	15.11.18	09.00	General Parades etc.	Lt Col E.P.Lloyd D.S.O.
	16.11.18	09.00	do do do	rejoined Bn
	17.11.18	09.00	Battalion Church Parade.	Lt A. Carman M.C.
	18.11.18	09.00	General Parades etc.	rejoined Bn
	19.11.18	09.15	The Battalion went for a short Route March.	
		11.30	The Batln Education Officer lectured to Officers W.O's N.C.O's and men of A.& B. Coys on the Demobilization Scheme. All the factors and	Bn Educ Officer
		12.15	difficulties governing demobilization were explained. The Battn Education Officer explained more fully the demobilization scheme to all Officers W.O's and N.C.O's of the Battalion.	Capt J. Dawson M.C.
	20.11.18	09.00	General inspection Parades etc.	
		11.30	The Battn Education Officer lectured to all ranks of C.& D. Coys on the demobilization scheme. Result of Final Inter- Company Football Competition. C. Coy .. 6. B. Coy ... Nil.	
	21.11.18	09.00	General inspection parades etc.	
		10.15	Lieut M.O. Perrins lectured to all ranks of A. Coy on the Education scheme, and to all ranks of B. Coy at 11-30 hours. The men displayed	
		11.30		
		14.00	interest in the scheme. Football Match. Officers 1st Battn Lincolnshire Regt V Officers 2nd Bn Lincolnshire Regt This match was played on the 1st Bn Lincolnshire Regt recreation ground and aroused considerable interest. Result:- 1st Bn Lincolnshire Regt 1 .. 2nd Bn Lincolnshire Regt. 1. Lieut M.O. Perrins lectured to all ranks of C. Company on the Education scheme.	
	22.11.18	09.30		
	23.11.18		The Battn bathed at AYMERIES.	

Army Form C. 2118.

WAR DIARY
or
INTELLIGENCE SUMMARY.
(Erase heading not required.)

Place	Date	Hour	Summary of Events and Information	Remarks and references to Appendices
BACHANT	22.11.18		The result of the Inter-Company Competition in Billets, Guards and Cookers over a period of twelve (12) days. B. Coy 1st A. Coy 2nd C. Coy 3rd D. Coy 4th.	Ref Sheet 51. 2/Lt G.R. Chark awarded M.C.
	23.11.18	09.15	The Battalion went for a Route March to LIMONT-FONTAINE and back via AULNOYE.	Capt J.P. Clingo M.C. rej from Hosp.
	24.11.18	11.00	Battalion attended a Church Parade in a factory at ETREE (U.17.c.6.)	2/Lt W.E. Deavin rej from Hosp.
		14.30	Football Match :- Officers V W.O's and Sgts. Result Officers 1. W.O's and Sgts. 6.	
	25.11.18	09.15	Battn went on a Route March to LIMONT - FONTAINE and back via St REMY.	Lt J.S. Carr & Lt B. Middleton
	26.11.18	09.00	General Parades etc.	joined Bn and posted to B. Coy.
		11.00	Battn Ceremonial Parade under Comg Officer.	
		12.5	Education Officer lectured to D. Coy on the representation of People act. The organisation and way of voting at home when absent was explained.	
	27.11.18	14.30	The same lecture was given to A.& B. Coys.	
		09.00	General Parades etc. Armourer Sgt inspected Rifles, Lewis Guns, and revolvers of A. Coy and at 14-00 hours B. Coy.	
		11.00	Commanding Officer inspected the Lewis Guns of C.& D. Coys.	
		12.00	Capt J.P. Clingo M.C. lectured to N.C.O's on MARCHING ORDER	
		06.00	Advance Party under Capt J.P. Clingo M.C. proceeded to new area.	
	28.11.18	09.00	General Parades etc.	2/Lt D.B. Sowerby joined Bn and posted to C. Coy.
		11.00	Commanding Officer inspected the Lewis Guns of Bn Hd Qrs and A.& B. Coys Lewis Guns and revolvers of C. Coy.	2/Lt O. Gray joined Bn and posted to B. Coy
	29.11.18	09.00	Armourer Sgt inspected Rifles Lewis Guns and revolvers of D. Coy.	
		11.00	General Parades etc.	
		11.00	Armourer Sgt inspected Rifles of D. Coy.	
		11.00	Battn Ceremonial Parade.	

E.M. Lloyd
Lieut Colonel
Commanding 2nd Bn Lincolnshire Regiment.

APPENDIX I

1st BATTⁿ THE LINCOLNSHIRE REGIMENT

OPERATION ORDER No. 158
— by —
LT. COL. N. M. S. IRWIN D.S.O. M.C. Commdg.

REF. 57 B.N.E.
    51 A. S.E.
    51 A. S.W.

No. 14
3-11-18

1. The Bn. will move to Concentration 'D' as follows tomorrow:—
Order of march Bn. H.Q. 'A' 'B' 'C' 'D'
Starting Point Cross Roads F. 7. d. 7. 3.
Time 1310 hours
200 yard distance between Coys
Route will be detailed tomorrow

DISTRIBUTION
as for O/O 157

Capt. & Adjt
1 Bn. The Lincolnshire
Regt.

1st BATTn THE LINCOLNSHIRE REGIMENT

OPERATION ORDER No 157
— by —
LT. COL. N.M.S. IRWIN D.S.O. M.C Commdg.

REF. 51 S.W. 1/20000

No 14
3-11-18

1 The First French, Fourth Third & First British Armies will resume the offensive to-morrow 4th Nov. 1918

The V Corps in conjunction will attack with 38th Division on Right, 17th Division on Left as far as GREEN line

The 33rd Division on Right & 21st Division on Left will pass through on 5th inst. to BLACK, YELLOW & BROWN dotted lines

The attack of 21st Division will be carried out as follows

    62nd Bde. -------- BLACK line
    64th " -------- YELLOW line
    110th " -------- BROWN dotted line

The attack of 62nd Bde. will be carried out by 12/13th N.Fs on Right, 1st Lincolns on Left, 2nd Lincolns in support.

The attack will be without a barrage on advanced Guard principles

The objectives & boundaries are shown on Map issued to Coys.

2 The attack of the Battalion from GREEN LINE will be carried out as follows:—

Time of leaving GREEN line 06.30 hours 5th inst. the advance being governed by Roads

'B' Coy. Road through T.15. Central to E. edge of uncut forest through T.22.a. & T.16.d

'A' Coy. Railway through T.16. & T.17. to BLACK line

'C' Coy Railway to T.15.b.7.5. thence E. along N. edge of uncut forest to Road at T.16.b.1.9. thence along Road through LA GRANDE CARRIERE to BLACK LINE

'D' Coy. Two platoons follow 'C' Coy. & establish a defensive flank & liaison post at cross Roads T.11.c.3.1.
'D' Coy. less two platoons move in support of 'C' Coy. to E. end of LA GRANDE CARRIERE

The advance of B, A & C Coys. respectively will be covered by an advanced Guard of one platoon

Distance between advanced Guard and main body of Coy. 300 yards

Picquets on roads through forest will be established as follows:—

'B' Coy.   1 platoon   T.22.a.9.7.
           1 platoon   T.16.d.5.5.
'D' Coy.   1 platoon   T.16.b.8.8.

On capture of BLACK LINE 'B' Coy. less 2 platoons (Picquets) will move forward in to Spurr in T.17.c in support of 'A' Coy.

'D' Coy. less 3 platoons (picquets & liason Post) will be support of 'C' Coy. at W. end of LA CARRIERE

On capture of BLACK LINE 'A' & 'C' Coys. will push forward a fighting Patrol (1 platoon) to R. SAMBRE to exploit success & make good any crossings in the Bn. frontage. These Patrols will only pursue a retreatory enemy who is offering no opposition

'A' & 'C' Coys. will move up in support of Patrols when reports are received that no opposition has been encountered as far as River.

N.B. 'C' Coy. will first ensure the mopping up of LA GRAND CARRIERE as far as T.13. central

3. Routes & Preliminary Concentrations to GREEN line as follows:—

Concentration 'D' X.29. & 30 Time of Arrival
                                             14.30 hours 4th inst.
Concentration 'B' S.16.b.   Time of Arrival
                                             1700 hours 4th inst.

Move from Concentration 'B' as follows:—
Order of March A, B, C, D, Bn. HQ.
Starting Point cross Roads S.17.b.7.7.
Time   0400 hours

Route Starting Point — Route de FLAQUETTE to S.18.d.6.0. thence E.N.E. along SENTIER ST. HUBERT to Railway. 'B' Coy. will turn off down Road running S.E. at T.14.b.5.6.

Advanced Guard formation will be adopted by 'A' Coy. from starting Point.
         'B' Coy. from Point where 'B' Coy. turns S.E. at T.14.b.5.6.

200 yards distance between Coys. will be maintained till head of Bn. reaches GREEN line when attack distances will be taken up.

Times & Routes at which Bn. moves from VENDIGIES & Concentration 'D' will be issued under separate order

4. DRESS   Fighting order

5. TRANSPORT   The following transport will
              accompany Bn. as far as Concentration
              'B'
              2 cookers
              Water cart
              Mess cart
              Mallise cart
              2 L.G. limbers
            * 3 Pack animals with tools
            * Chargers
                    * will accompany Bn.
                      throughout advance

6. Teas will be issued at Concentration 'D'
   & 'B'. Rations for 5th inst. issued at Concentration
   'B'

7. 1 Section R.F.A., 1 Section M.G., 2 L.T.M.S. will
   be attached to Bn. 1 Section M.G. will move
   independently to a position on high ground
   in T.22.b & T.17.c. after capture of BLACK line
   & further orders will be issued to O.C. M.G. Section

8. Bn. H.Q. as follows:-
        Concentration 'B' road junction S.16.a.2.4.
        GREEN line   Saw Mill   T.9.c.7.0
        During advance on BLACK line Bn. H.Q.
        will adhere to line of Railway

9. R.A.P. & Prisoners Post at Bn. H.Q.

10. The Bn. will be prepared to take part in
    attack on any objectives not captured by
    17th Division

11. A two minute crash to signal ZERO will
    be put down by artillery at following points
    at 0630 hours
            T.15.d.7.5
            T.15.b.7.5
            T.16.b.1.9

ACKNOWLEDGE

DISTRIBUTION
1 C.O.   8 R.S.M.
2 O/c A Coy   8a 1st E.SURREYS (5th Div)
3 - B -   9 62nd L.T.M.
4 - C -   10 21st Dn M.G.
5 - D -   11 12/S N.F.
6 - G.M.   12 62 Infy Bde
7 - T.O   13 FILE
                 14&15 WAR DIARY

Capt & Adjt

Confidential

WAR DIARY (Volume 12)

of

2nd Bn Lincolnshire Regiment

for period

1st December 1918

to

31st December 1918.

EPLloyd Lieut Colonel
Commdg 2nd Bn Lincolnshire Regt.

3.1.19.

Army Form C. 2118.

WAR DIARY
or
INTELLIGENCE SUMMARY.
(Erase heading not required.)

Instructions regarding War Diaries and Intelligence Summaries are contained in F. S. Regs., Part II. and the Staff Manual respectively. Title pages will be prepared in manuscript.

Place	Date	Hour	Summary of Events and Information	Remarks and references to Appendices
BACHANT	1.12.18	11.00	Battalion Church Parade in Divisional Theatre at ETREE (U 17.a.6.7.)	Ref. 51. 1/40,000.
"	2.12.18	09.00	General Parades and recreation.	
"	3.12.18	08.45	Battalion marched to PONT-SUR-SAMBRE to await the arrival of His Majesty The King.	
"		10.35	His Majesty The King, His Royal Highness The Prince of Wales and Prince Albert passed through PONT-SUR-SAMBRE walking. The 62nd Infantry Brigade who were assembled in the square gave the Royal party a most hearty reception.	
"	4.12.18	09.00	General Parades etc.	2/Lt H.Parrish Joined Battn and is posted B.Coy.
"		14.15	Football match:- Battalion v 63rd Field Ambulance, Result Bn 1 63 1 Field Amb. 1.oo Nil.	2/Lt W.A.S.Whipp Appointed Battn Caterer.
"	5.12.18	11.00	Bn Parades under Company Officer.	2/Lt P.H.Broom rej from Hosp.and posted to D.Coy.
"	6.11.18	07.45	Lieut J.S.Carr proceeded to CAMBRAI in charge of the miners who were being released from military service to take up their civilian occupation.	
"	7.12.18	11.00	Battalion Pur'e under Adjutant.	
"		14.30	Football Match:- Officers v W.O's & Sergts. Result Officers 3. W.O's & Sergts 1.	
"		18.00	Lincolnshire Poachers (Bn Concert Party) gave performance in the Divisional Theatre at ETREE.	
"	8.12.18	11.00	General Church Parade in Divisional Theatre at ETREE.	
"	9.12.18	09.00	General Parades and recreation.	
"		12.00	Riding class under Transport Officer for all Officers of A.&B.Coys.	
"	10.12.18	09.00	General Parades etc.	
"	11.12.18	09.00	General Inspection Parades etc.	
"	12.12.18	08.45	Party under Capt. E.P.O. Richards M.C. proceeded to Bermai to fetch the COLOURS from LINCOLN.	
"		09.00	General Parades etc.	
"		17.15	A Battalion Whist Drive was held and was greatly appreciated by all ranks.	
"	13.12.18	09.00	General Parades etc.	
"	14.12.18	09.30	Commanding Officer lectured all Company Commanders in Marching Order.	
"		11.40	Lieut M.O.Perrins lectured all Officers on "BRITISH CONSTITUTION" on "MACHINERY of GOVERNMENT".	

Army Form C. 2118.

WAR DIARY
or
INTELLIGENCE SUMMARY.
(Erase heading not required.)

Instructions regarding War Diaries and Intelligence Summaries are contained in F. S. Regs., Part II. and the Staff Manual respectively. Title pages will be prepared in manuscript.

Place	Date	Hour	Summary of Events and Information	Remarks and references to Appendices
BACHANT	14.12.18	14.00	Regimental Sports were amused held and aroused considerable interest	
		18.00	"Lincolnshire Poachers" gave a performance in the Divisional Theatre at ETREE. The concert was a great success.	
"	15.12.18	11.00	Church Parade in Divisional Theatre.	
"	16.12.18	09.00	General Parades and preparations for moving on the next Day.	
"	17.12.18	07.00	62nd Infantry Bde commenced movement to new area and proceeded by route march to ENGLE-FONTAINE in the following order:— 1st Battn Lincolnshire Regiment. 2nd Battn Lincolnshire Regiment.	Ref 1/100000 V_____12.
		07.15	12/13. Northumberland Fusiliers. Billeting Party proceeded on bicycles to ENGLE-FONTAINE.	
		10.45	The Battalion marching through AULNOYE & BERG AIMONT, the Battalion halted at LOCQUINOL and Had The _____ _____	
		12.00	March was resumed	
		13.30	Battalion reached ENGLE-FONTAINE and moved _____ _____ _____ _____	
ENGLE-FONTAINE	18.12.18	06.45	62nd Infantry Bde resumed march _____ _____ _____ in the following order. 2nd Bn Lincolnshire Regiment. 12/13th Northumberland Fusiliers. 1st Bn Lincolnshire Regiment. Route ... ENGLE-FONTAINE, CROIX, FOREST-MONTAY, INCHY.	
		07.00	Billeting party proceeded on bicycles to INCHY.	
INCHY		11.05	Battn reached INCHY and moved into billets for the night. Throughout the two days march the weather and roads conditions were	Ref V _____ 1/100000.
"	19.12.18	06.00	bad, but all ranks marched well. Battalion embussed.	
		06.45	The journey was resumed by bus to the CAVILLON area. Route ... INCHY. CAMBRAI. BAPAUME. ALBERT. AMIENS. BRIQUEMESNIL.	Ref 1/100000 Amiens 17.
SAISSEVAL		07.00	62nd Infantry Bde Transport resumed march to SAISSEVAL and moved	
		17.00	Battalion debussed at BRIQUEMESNIL and marched to SAISSEVAL and moved into prepared billets. D.Coy took over billets in SAISSEMONT.	
"	20.12.18		Battalion Rested.	

Army Form C. 2118.

WAR DIARY
or
INTELLIGENCE SUMMARY.
(Erase heading not required.)

Instructions regarding War Diaries and Intelligence Summaries are contained in F. S. Regs., Part II. and the Staff Manual respectively. Title pages will be prepared in manuscript.

Place	Date	Hour	Summary of Events and Information	Remarks and references to Appendices
SAISSEVAL	21.12.18		Battalion rested and cleaned up.	
	22.12.18	11.00	Voluntary Church Parade.	
	23.12.18	09.00	General parade.	
		20.00	Party under Capt. E.P.C. McMurtrie M.C. paraded for X'mas tree in COLOURS.	Capt. J. Dawson M.C. apptd Education Offr.
	24.12.18	09.00	General parade.	Lt M.D. Perrins apptd Demobilization Offr.
	25.12.18		Christmas Day.	2/Lt J. Wilson apptd Billet & Fire Offr.
			The Pioneers decorated the Theatre & 3 Pumping Sergts' Mess, also Quarter Masters, Sergts. Mess etc. The Commanding Officer visited every Mess and wished the men a Happy X'mas. Dinner and everything was very successful. The Battn Orchestra played at the mens messes.	
	26.12.18	14.30	Football match:- Officers v W.O.'s & Sergts. Result Officers 2. W.O's & Sergts 4.	
	27.12.18	09-15	Battalion Route March. Route:- SAISSEVAL. BRIQUEMESNIL. FLOXICOURT. BOUGAINVILLE. FLUY. PISSY. BOVELLES.	
	28.12.18	09.00	General Inspection Parades etc.	
	29.12.18	08.30	Voluntary Church Services in the school	
		17.30	" " " "	
	30.12.18	09.00	Drill Parades, P.T. & G. Instruction	
	31.12.18	09.00	C.O.'s Parade for I G instruction of J.N.C.O.'s of "A" & "B" Coys Lieut Col I.W. Berry Commdg O.C. Officers "A" & "B" Coys	

(signature)

Lieut Colonel.
Commanding 2nd Battn Lincolnshire Regiment.

<u>Confidential.</u>

<u>War Diary</u> (Volume 1)

of the

<u>2nd Battn Lincolnshire Regt</u>

for period

<u>1st January 1919</u>

to

<u>31st January 1919.</u>

W Hoyd Lieut Colonel.
Commdg 2nd Bn Lincs Regt.

Army Form C. 2118.

WAR DIARY
or
INTELLIGENCE SUMMARY.
(Erase heading not required.)

Instructions regarding War Diaries and Intelligence Summaries are contained in F.S. Regs., Part II. and the Staff Manual respectively. Title pages will be prepared in manuscript.

Place	Date	Hour	Summary of Events and Information	Remarks and references to Appendices
SAISSEVAL	1.1.19	09.45	The Battn. was formed up in a field West of SAISSEMONT to receive the Bde. Commander (Brig. Gen. G.H.GATER. C.M.G. D.S.O.) who was paying his farewell visit to the Battalion.	
		10.00	The Bde. commander armed made an admirable speech in which he thanked all ranks for the magnificent work they had done, especially during the six great battles from Aug 21st 1918 to Novr 11th 1918.	
			The Commanding Officer (Lt Col E.R.LLOYD. D.S.O.) replied and the Guard was given three ring hearty cheers.	
"	2.1.19	09.00	General parade, recreation & Lewis Guns instruction.	
		10.30	Class formed for men who wish to become proficient in Morse Code.	
		14.30	A series of Battn. Whist Drives was begun, with great success.	
		18.00	The "Kinematic Pierrots" gave a concert in the Battalion theatre. It was proposed to give a concert every night.	
"	3.1.19	09.00	General parade, recreation & Lewis Guns instruction.	
		10.30	Morse Code Class.	
		17.30	Battalion Whist Drive.	

Army Form C. 2118.

WAR DIARY
or
INTELLIGENCE SUMMARY.
(Erase heading not required.)

Instructions regarding War Diaries and Intelligence Summaries are contained in F. S. Regs., Part II. and the Staff Manual respectively. Title pages will be prepared in manuscript.

Place	Date	Hour	Summary of Events and Information	Remarks and references to Appendices
SAISSEVAL	3.1.19	18.00	"Lincolnshire Poachers" gave a concert in Battn Theatre. All ranks thoroughly enjoyed the performance.	
"	4.1.19	09.00	General parade, recreation & Lewis Gun instruction. "A" Company commence cleaning Battn. Area of wire and pickets.	
		10.30	Mens hair clean.	
		14.30	A series of Shorthand classes were commenced.	
		17.30	An inter-platoon football league was commenced.	
		18.00	Battn. Whist Drive. Suppers was provided after the play.	
		18.00	"Lincolnshire Poachers" gave a concert in the Battalion Theatre.	
"	5.1.19	10.00	Church Service in Battn. Theatre	
		14.30	Football Match - Battn v 21st Div M.T. Coy. Result:- Battn 0 - 21 Div M T Coy 7.	
"	6.1.19	09.00	General parade, recreation & Lewis Gun instruction.	
			"C" Company continued to clear Battn. Area of wire and pickets.	
		10.30	Shorthand and Morse code classes	
		14.30	Battn. Whist Drive	
		18.00	"Lincolnshire Poachers" gave a concert	

Army Form C. 2118.

WAR DIARY
or
INTELLIGENCE SUMMARY.
(Erase heading not required.)

Instructions regarding War Diaries and Intelligence Summaries are contained in F. S. Regs., Part II. and the Staff Manual respectively. Title pages will be prepared in manuscript.

Place	Date	Hour	Summary of Events and Information	Remarks and references to Appendices
SAISSEVAL	7-1-19	09.00	General parade, inspection and instruction in Lewis Gunnery	
		10.30	Horse bath and Boathard Classes	
		17.30	Batn. Whist Drive	
"	8-1-19	09.45	Batn. marched to BOVELLES and formed up in a large hangar together with the 12/13th Bn NORTHUMBERLAND FUSILIERS.	
		10.30	The Divisional Commander (Maj Gen. SIR D. CAMPBELL K.C.B. D.S.O.) arrived and addressed the two Battalions. The General Roushall paid for the magnificent work they had done and that the glorious reputation of the 38 Division he maintained. He further jointly be raised three hearty cheers for the 21st Division and for those who had died whilst upholding the honour of the Division. Lt. Col. E.F. LLOYD D.S.O. replied and called for cheers for the Divisional Commander, all ranks replies enthusiastically.	
		17.30	Batn. Whist Drive	
		18.00	Performance by "Curiosities" Concert in Battn. Theatre	
"	9-1-19	09.00	General parade, inspection and Lewis gun instruction	
		10.30	Skirmishing and Horse Exercises	

MAJ. W.H.E.QUATER
D.S.O. M.C. &c
No. 3 O Course
ALDERSHOT

Army Form C. 2118.

WAR DIARY
or
INTELLIGENCE SUMMARY.
(Erase heading not required.)

Instructions regarding War Diaries and Intelligence Summaries are contained in F. S. Regs., Part II. and the Staff Manual respectively. Title pages will be prepared in manuscript.

Place	Date	Hour	Summary of Events and Information	Remarks and references to Appendices
CAISSEVAL	9.1.19	19.30	Battn Whist Drive.	
		18.00	Performance by "Frivolities" Parties.	
	10.1.19	09.00	Mutual parades, rendezvous & Lewis gun instruction.	
			"D" Company continued to clean Br area of wire and pickets	
		10.00	Divisional Cross Country Race was held. The Battn Team were not successful in winning the race.	
		10.30	Minor Cadre & Shorthand classes.	
		17.30	Battn Whist Drive.	
		18.00	Performance by "Frivolities" Parties.	
	11.1.19	09.30	Inspection of Box Respirators, clothing and equipment.	
		09.30	The Commanding Officers inspected billets of transport, H.Q. & "D" Company	
		10.30	Minor Cadre & Shorthand classes.	
		17.30	Battn Whist Drive.	
		18.00	Performance by "Frivolities" Parties.	
	12.1.19		Church Parade Service in Cinema Theatre.	
	13.1.19	09.00	Special parade instruction & Lewis gun instruction. "D" Company continued to clean	Regt Band joined Battn from IRELAND
			Battn area of wire and pickets	
		10.30	Shorthand & Minor Cadre classes.	

Army Form C. 2118.

WAR DIARY
or
INTELLIGENCE SUMMARY.
(Erase heading not required.)

Instructions regarding War Diaries and Intelligence Summaries are contained in F. S. Regs., Part II. and the Staff Manual respectively. Title pages will be prepared in manuscript.

Place	Date	Hour	Summary of Events and Information	Remarks and references to Appendices
SAISSEVAL	13/1/19	14.20	Football Match - Batts v 1st Bn WILTSHIRE REGT. This match was played in the divisional competition and aroused great interest.	
			Result: Batt. 0 : 1st Bn WILTSHIRE REGT 4	
		17.30	Batta. Whist Drive.	
		19.00	Sing-song Concert in Batta. Theatre.	
"	14/1/19	09.00	Gas and passive protection & Lewis Gun instruction. "D" Coy resumed to-day	CAPT. DAWKINS M.C. rejoins Battn.
			Batta. Area.	
		10.30	Musing Cadre & Shorthand classes.	
		17.30	Batta. Whist Drive.	
			Band gave an orchestral concert in Bn. Theatre. The concert was greatly appreciated by all ranks.	
"	15.1.19	09.00	General Parades, recreation & Lewis Gun instruction "B" Company continued to clear Bn Area	
		10.30	Nursing Cadre & Shorthand classes.	
		17.30	Batta. Whist Drive.	
"	16.1.19	09.00	General parades, recreation & Lewis Gun instruction	

Army Form C. 2118.

WAR DIARY
or
INTELLIGENCE SUMMARY.
(Erase heading not required.)

Instructions regarding War Diaries and Intelligence Summaries are contained in F. S. Regs., Part II. and the Staff Manual respectively. Title pages will be prepared in manuscript.

Place	Date	Hour	Summary of Events and Information	Remarks and references to Appendices
BAISSEVAL	16/1/19	10.30	Shorthand and Morse to the Classes	
			Brigade Commander inspected Batty transport and Batts billets	
		17.30	Battn Whist Drive	
		18.00	Performance by Lancashire Lasses	
	17/1/19	09.00	House - of printers, recreation & lewis gun instruction	
		10.30	"B" Company continued to clear Bath Area	
			Shorthand typewriting Classes closed	
		17.30	Battn Whist Drive	
		18.00	Performance by Lancashire Lasses	
"	18.1.19	Open	Inspection of Boot Repairing, clothing & equipment	
		10.00	"D" Coy bathed at Bath Estbt.	
		10.30	Shorthand, Morse Code Classes	
		17.30	Battn Whist Drive	
		18.00	"Lancashire Lasses" gave another successful performance.	
"	19.1.19	10.00	Church parade service in B.E. Theatre.	
		11.00	Regtl Band played selections	
		18.00	Orchestral concert in Theatre.	

Army Form C. 2118.

WAR DIARY
or
INTELLIGENCE SUMMARY.
(Erase heading not required.)

Place	Date	Hour	Summary of Events and Information	Remarks and references to Appendices
SAISSEVAL	20.1.1909.00		General parade, inspection of Lewis Guns, instruction "A" Company employment	
			to clear Bath Area.	
		10.30	Shorthand and Morse Code classes.	
			Tug of war — Bath v. 1st Bn WILTSHIRE REGT.	
			This tug of war was in the Divisional Competition. Result: Bn 1 pull - 1st Bn WILTSHIRE	
			REGT. 2 pulls.	
"	21.1.1909.00		General parade, recreation & Lewis Gun instruction "A" Coy continued to clear	
			Bath Area.	
		10.0 a	"B" Coy bathed at Bath bath.	
		10.30	Shorthand & Morse Code classes.	
		17.30	Bath Whist Drive	
		18.00	Performance by "Kiwiosties Pierrots"	
			Total number of Other ranks already demobilised from Battn.	
			(a) Miners 98. (b) Guarantee Letters men 46. (c) Pivotal men 26.	
			(d) Men over 41 years old 6. (e) Men over 41 years old 6, (e) Demobilized on leave 19, (f) Groups 32,	
			(g) Long Service 16, (h) Serving Soldiers 9. Total 252.	

Army Form C. 2118.

WAR DIARY
of
INTELLIGENCE SUMMARY.
(Erase heading not required.)

Instructions regarding War Diaries and Intelligence Summaries are contained in F. S. Regs., Part II. and the Staff Manual respectively. Title pages will be prepared in manuscript.

Place	Date	Hour	Summary of Events and Information	Remarks and references to Appendices
SAISSEVAL	22.1.19	9.0	General parades, meetings & lewis gun instruction	
		10.00	"B" Coy continued to clean Bath area	
		10.00	"A" Coy bathed at Saisseval Baths	
		10.30	Horse back & shorthand classes	
		11.30	Baths. Wheat Drive	
		18.00	Performance by Divisional Pierrots	
	23.1.19	0900	General parades, meetings & lewis gun instruction. "D" Coy continues to clean Bath area	
		10.00	Regimentally employed men bathed in Saisseval baths	
		10.30	Shorthand & horse back classes	
		11.30	Baths. Wheat Drive. A team of 16 represented each Coy and the Quartermaster Officers gave prizes to the winning team.	
	24.1.1909	9.0	General parades, meetings & lewis gun instruction. "D" Coy continues to clean Bath area	
		10.00	"A" Coy bathed at Baths	
		10.30	Horse back & Shorthand classes	
		18.00	Performance by "Lancashire Pierrots"	

Army Form C. 2118.

WAR DIARY
or
INTELLIGENCE SUMMARY.
(Erase heading not required.)

Place	Date	Hour	Summary of Events and Information	Remarks and references to Appendices
SAISSEVAL	25.1.19	09.00	General parade recreation & Lewis gun instruction, "C" Coy continued to clean the Rattn area of mud & rubish.	
		18.00	Performance by "Curiduson Scales"	
	26.1.19	10.00	Church parade service in Rattn Theatre	
	27.1.19	09.00	General inspection parade & recreation "C" Coy continued to clean Battn area	
		11.00	The Brigade Commander lectured to all officers & other ranks of "A" "B" & "D" Company the subject of the lecture was a true story of human progress from primitive man; all ranks were greatly interested.	
		17.30	Run whist drive in Battn Recreation Room	
	28.1.19	09.00	General parade recreation & Lewis gun instruction "C" Coy continued to clean Rattn area.	
		10.30	Short handwritten bode classes.	
			So as not in the history education of officers likely to remain in the Post Bellum Army a series of lectures were begun under Lt.Col. arrangement. Lect (6) officers of the Battn attended.	

Army Form C. 2118.

WAR DIARY
or
INTELLIGENCE SUMMARY.
(Erase heading not required.)

Place	Date	Hour	Summary of Events and Information	Remarks and references to Appendices
SAISSEVAL	19.1.19	09.30	Batt. route march Roads:- SEUX - BOVELLES. The Batt. halted North of BOVELLES and a cross country race to SAISSEVAL was arranged. All ranks competed with enthusiasm & the Commanding Officer gave prize to the various winners.	
		18.00	Another very successful performance by the "Lincolnshire Lassies"	
	20.1.19	09.00	General parade, recreation & Lewis gun instruction	
		10.30	Shorthand Morse Code classes	
		11.45	Major E.C. KEMPE, C.F. lectured to the Battn. on AUSTRALIA	
		18.00	The "STAR" (V Corps) concert party gave a very enjoyable concert in the Batth. Theatre.	
	21.1.19	09.00	General parades, recreation & Lewis gun instruction.	
		10.30	Morse Code & Shorthand Classes	
		18.00	Performance by "STAR" concert party in Battn. Theatre.	
			Men demobilized from 21.1.19:-	
			Serving soldiers 10, Pivotal men 5, Grenades between 39, over 41, 1,	
			Long service 4. Repatriated 1, Group 1, 27, Group 30, 3, Group 35, 1. Group 3/5, 1.	

E.M. Lloyd Lieut Colonel
Commanding 2nd Bn Lincolnshire Regt.

Confidential. 38

War Diary

of the

2nd Bn Lincolnshire Regt

for period

1st February 1919

to

28th February 1919

(Volume 2)

CMoyl Lieut Colonel.
Commdg 2nd Bn Lincolnshire Regt.

WAR DIARY
or
INTELLIGENCE SUMMARY.
(Erase heading not required.)

Army Form C. 2118.

Instructions regarding War Diaries and Intelligence Summaries are contained in F.S. Regs., Part II. and the Staff Manual respectively. Title pages will be prepared in manuscript.

Place	Date	Hour	Summary of Events and Information	Remarks and references to Appendices
SAISSEVAL	1-2-19	09.00	General parades, recreation & Lewis Gun instruction	
		10.30	Shorthand & Morse Code Classes	
		17.30	The "STAR" (v/Bn) concert party gave a performance in the Battn. Theatre	
	2-2-19	10.00	Church Service in Battn. Theatre	
	3-2-19	09.00	General parades, recreation & Lewis Gun instruction	
		10.30	Shorthand & Morse code classes	
		18.00	Performance by Punchers Kit Crackers Concert Party	
	4-2-19	09.00	General parades, recreation and Lewis Gun Instruction	
		10.30	Shorthand & Morse code classes	
		17.30	An Inter-Coy tug of War Tournament was held on the Battn. recreation ground. Officers and all ranks enjoyed the Evening.	
	5-2-19	09.00	General Parades, recreation & Lewis Gun instruction	
		10.00	A lecture on "Military Law" was attended by six (6) Officers of the Battn. Major LYNDON gave the lecture at FOURDRINOY	
		10.30	Shorthand & Morse code classes	
		18.00	The Lincolns Kit Crackers Gave their farewell concert in the Battn. Theatre. After the performance the Commanding Officer, from the stage, thanked the Concert Party for the very enjoyable concerts they had given and presented a Silver Match box to each of the three principal oldest members of the party.	
	6-2-19	09.00	General parades & recreation.	
		11.00	Bde Commander talked to the Battn. on single times, he described the rise and fall of Greece, Rome, the Carthaginians & finally brought us to the baseline of William the Conqueror & HASTINGS. All ranks were greatly interested.	

Army Form C. 2118.

WAR DIARY
or
INTELLIGENCE SUMMARY.
(Erase heading not required.)

Instructions regarding War Diaries and Intelligence
Summaries are contained in F. S. Regs., Part II.
and the Staff Manual respectively. Title pages
will be prepared in manuscript.

Place	Date	Hour	Summary of Events and Information	Remarks and references to Appendices
SAISSEVAL	6-2-19	18.00	The "CHEERY O'Donart Party" (V/t Corps HART) gave a performance in the Battn Theatre	
"	7-2-19	09.00	General parade, inspection & Lewis Gun instructions	
		10.30	Short hand & horse cold classes	
"	8-2-19	18.00	Concert by "CHEERY O" concert Party in Bn Theatre	
"	9-2-19	10.00	Church Parade. Service in Battn Theatre.	
"	10-2-19	09.00	A & B Coys General Parades revolver and Lewis Gun instruction	
			C & D Coys continued to clear Bn Area	
"	11-2-19	09.30	Bn Route March.	
			Route:— BOVELLES — FERRIERS — J.22.d.25.65 SAISSEVAL.	
"	12-2-19	09.00	A & B Coys General parades & Lewis Gun Instruction	Reg Strength 62 & 1/20.00
			C & D Coys continued to clear Battn Area.	
		11.00	Confirmation Service by the Bishop of Leicester in Battn Church Hut.	
"	13-2-19	09.00	A & B Coys General parades, revolver & Lewis Gun Instructions	
			C & D Coys continued to clear Battn Area.	
"	14-2-19	09.30	Battn Route March.	
			Route:— FOURDRINOY — J.8.d.5.8 — L.6.d.5.9 — CAVILLON — FOURDRINOY — SAISSEVAL.	
			At J.8.d.5.8. the Battn joined the other Battns of the 62nd Inf Bde and from this point to CAVILLON it was a Bde Route March. The Brigade halted at L.6.d.5.9. for 20 minutes & the Bde Comm ander having called all Officers out asked a few questions on tactics route marching subjects.	
"	15-2-19	09.00	Coy inspections of Boots, washing, clothing and equipment	
		10.00	The Commanding Officer inspected huts of HD Coy & the Band.	
"	16-2-19	11.00	Church parade. Service in Battn Theatre.	

(10340) Wt W5304/1715 750,000 3/18 E 2688 Forms/C2118/6.

Army Form C. 2118.

WAR DIARY
or
INTELLIGENCE SUMMARY.
(Erase heading not required.)

Instructions regarding War Diaries and Intelligence Summaries are contained in F. S. Regs., Part II. and the Staff Manual respectively. Title pages will be prepared in manuscript.

Place	Date	Hour	Summary of Events and Information	Remarks and references to Appendices
SAISSEVAL	17-2-19	09.00	General Parade & inspection	
		09.30	Commanding Officer inspected A. Coy.	
		10.00	Commanding Officer inspected B. Coy.	
	18-2-19	09.45	Battn. Route March. Route :- SEUX - FLUY - 0.22 d 3.5 - FLOXICOURT - BRIQUEMESNIL - SAISSEVAL.	
	19-2-19	09.30	Lewis Gun Officers inspected Lewis Guns & spare parts of A. Coy.	
			Commanding Officer inspected A. Coy.	
			Commanding Officer inspected B. Coy.	
	20-2-19	14.00	Lewis Gun Officer inspected & checked Lewis Guns & spare parts of B. Coy.	
		09.30	Commanding Officer inspected D. Coy.	
		10.00	Commanding Officer inspected C. Coy.	
		11.30	Lewis Gun Officer inspected and checked Lewis Guns & spare parts of H.Q. and D. Coy.	
		14.30	Football Match inter-Company final Result C. Coy. 2 D. Coy. 1.	
	21-2-19	09.30	Bde. Route March. 62nd Inf. Bde. formed up at SAISSEVAL. Route :- Q.1.a.1.9 - J.23.a.6.1. SAISSEVAL. The Bde. halted at J.23 & carried out an advanced post scheme.	
	22-2-19	09.00	Coy inspections of clothing and equipment. Revolver Training.	
		10.00	Church Parade service in Battn. Theatre.	
		11.00	Battn. Orchestra gave a concert in Battn. Theatre.	
	24-2-19	09.00	General Parade & Inspection. D + B Coys. Bathed at Battn. Baths.	
	25-2-19	09.15	Battn. Route March. Route :- BOVELLES - PISSY - REVELLES - FLUY - BRIQUEMESNIL - SAISSEVAL.	

Army Form C. 2118.

WAR DIARY
or
INTELLIGENCE SUMMARY.

(Erase heading not required.)

Instructions regarding War Diaries and Intelligence Summaries are contained in F. S. Regs., Part II. and the Staff Manual respectively. Title pages will be prepared in manuscript.

Place	Date	Hour	Summary of Events and Information	Remarks and references to Appendices
SAISSEVAL	26.2.19	09.30	A & C Coys Bathed at Battn Baths.	
			B & B Coys continued work of filling in trenches.	
	27.2.19	09.30	A & C Coys general parades & reaction B & D " continued to fill in trenches	
"	28.2.19	09.00	Bde Route March. Battn moved off and joined the other Battns of the 62nd Bde at Bois de FOURDRINOY. ROUTE FOURDRINOY — CAVILLON — RIENCOURT — OISSY — CAVILLON — FOURDRINOY SAISSEVAL.	
		08.30	Army examination for 2nd Class certificate was held in the Battn Etmet Hut.	
		14.00	Army examination for 3rd Class certificate Nom au of O.R. Demobling et during February 1919. Guarantee Letters 99. Over 41. 2. Serving Soldiers 18. Long Service 28. AFZ 32. 14. AFZ 56. 3. Priority Groups 75. TOTAL 239.	

[signature] Lt. Col.
COMMDG 2ND BN LINCOLNSHIRE REGIMENT.

Secret

CONFIDENTIAL.

WAR DIARY

of the

2nd. Bn. LINCOLNSHIRE REGT.

for period

1st. MARCH 1919 to 31st. MARCH 1919.

VOLUME 3.

Hanway
Capt. & Adjt.
for O.C. 2nd. Bn. Lincolnshire Regiment.

Army Form C. 2118.

2nd.Bn.LINCOLNSHIRE REGIMENT.   WAR DIARY   VOLUME 3.

or INTELLIGENCE SUMMARY.

(Erase heading not required.)

Instructions regarding War Diaries and Intelligence Summaries are contained in F.S. Regs., Part II. and the Staff Manual respectively. Title pages will be prepared in manuscript.

Place	Date	Hour	Summary of Events and Information	Remarks and references to Appendices
SAISSEVAL.	1/3/19.	09.30.	A.C.& D.Coys continue to fill in trenches. B.Coy., general parades & recreation.	
	2	1100. 1145. 1330.	Church Parade Service in Battalion Theatre. Band played selections outside theatre. Battalion 6 a side Football competition.	
	3	0900.	General parades & recreation.	
	4	0930.	A.& C.Coys dismantled "B" football ground. D.Coy continued work on football ground. B.Coy general parades & recreation.	
	5	0930. 1215.	A.&C.Coys complete dismantling of "B" football ground. B.& D.Coys dismantle "A" football ground. 2/Lieut.W.E.Deavin proceeds to CAVILLON to prepare billets for B.H.Q., A.& C.Coys. 2/Lieut.W.Seadar proceeded to FOURDRINOY to prepare billets for "B"&"D"Coys.	
	6	1130 1345 1400	All stores dumped in Hospital Nissen hut & conveyed to new area by lorry. Bn Hqrs,Band, A.&B.Coys marched to CAVILLON & took over prepared billets. B.& D.Coys, Q.M.Stores & Transport march to FOURDRINOY & took over prepared billets.	
CAVILLON.	7	0900	General parades and recreation.	
	8	1000 1100 1430	Commanding Officer inspects billets of B.& D.Coys,Q.M.Stores& Transport. Commanding officer inspects billets of A.& C.Coys,Band & Bn Hqrs. Football match:- Battn(CAVILLON) v 62nd Inf.Bde.H.Q.. Result:.....Battn 1 Bde.H.Q. 2.	
	9			

Army Form C. 2118.

WAR DIARY
or
INTELLIGENCE SUMMARY.
(Erase heading not required.)

Volume 3.

2nd Bn Lincolnshire Regiment.

Instructions regarding War Diaries and Intelligence Summaries are contained in F. S. Regs., Part II. and the Staff Manual respectively. Title pages will be prepared in manuscript.

Place	Date	Hour	Summary of Events and Information	Remarks and references to Appendices
CAVILLON.	9/3/19	1000	Church Parade Service in Recreation room FOURDRINOY.	
		1430	Hockey Match:- Battn (CAVILLON) v Battn (FOURDRINOY) Result........ 4 .... 2.	
	10	0900	General Parades and Recreation.	
	11	0900	General Parades and Recreation.	
	12	0945	Battn Route March. Route:- CAVILLON-PICQUIGNY-FOURDRINOY-CAVILLON.	
	13	0900	General parades and Recreation.	
	14	0900	General Parades and Recreation.	
		1430	Hockey Match:- Battn v 1st Bn Lincolnshire Regt. Result.........5 ....1.	
	15	0900	General Parades and Recreation.	
		1030	O.R.s of Battn Cadre bath at PICQUIGNY Quarter Master checked Battn mobilisation stores at Corps Cadre Park LONGPRE.	
	16	1000	Church Parade Service in Recreation Room FOURDRINOY.	
	17	0900	General Parades and Recreation.	
	18	0900	General Parades and Recreation.	
	19	0900	General Parades and Recreation.	
	20	1100	Battn Bathing at PICQUIGNY.	

Army Form C. 2118.

2nd Bn Lincolnshire Regt.

WAR DIARY
or
INTELLIGENCE SUMMARY.

Volume 5.

(Erase heading not required.)

Instructions regarding War Diaries and Intelligence Summaries are contained in F. S. Regs., Part II. and the Staff Manual respectively. Title pages will be prepared in manuscript.

Place	Date	Hour	Summary of Events and Information	Remarks and references to Appendices
CAVILLON.	21/5/19	0900	General Parades and Recreation.	
	22	0900	General Parades and Recreation.	
	23	1100	Battn Band play selections at CAVILLON.	
	24	0900	General Parades and Recreation.	
	25	0900	General Parades and Recreation.	
	26	0900	General Parades and Recreation.	
		0900	First party of a draft 50 strong proceeded to AILLY-SUR-SOMME en route for 151st Prisoners of War Company. CALAIS.	
		1130	Remainder of draft proceed to AILLY-SUR-SOMME.	
	27	0900	General Parades and Recreation.	
	28	0900	General Parades and Recreation.	
		1100	Three officers (volunteers for the Army of Occupation) proceed to CALAIS to join the 151st Prisoners of War Company.	
	29	0900	General Parades and Recreation.	
	30	1100	Church Parade Service.	
		1130	Commanding Officer inspects B.& D.Coys.	
		1200	Commanding Officer inspects A.& C.Coys.	
	31	0900	General Parades and Recreation.	

Chawey
Captain & Adjutant,
2nd Bn. Lincolnshire Regiment.

3/21

1 Lincoln Regt

Vol ~~XII~~
XVIII
XVIII

62 Oct

3/21

1 Lincoln Regt
Vol 14

3/21

1 Lincoln Reg.t

Vol ~~XIII.~~

~~XVIII~~

~~XIX~~

www.ingramcontent.com/pod-product-compliance
Lightning Source LLC
Chambersburg PA
CBHW081534160426
43191CB00011B/1757